C·A·N·I·N·E

Massage

Also by Jean-Pierre Hourdebaigt

Equine Massage: A Practical Guide

C·A·N·I·N·E

Massage

A PRACTICAL GUIDE

JEAN-PIERRE HOURDEBAIGT, R.M.T.
AND
SHARI L. SEYMOUR, R.M.L.T.

HOWELL
BOOK HOUSE
NEW YORK

Some of the information in this book should be acted upon by experienced persons only. Furthermore, the book is not intended as a substitute for medical advice of licensed veterinarians. The information provided is for the purposes of education and to give a complete a picture as possible. The reader should regularly consult a veterinarian in matters relating to his or her dog's health and particularly in regard to any symptoms that may require diagnosis or medical attention.

Howell Book House
A Division of Macmillan General Reference
A Pearson Education Macmillan Company
1633 Broadway
New York, NY 10019-6785

Macmillan General Reference books may be purchased for business or sales promotional use. For information please write: Special Markets Department, Macmillan Publishing USA, 1633 Broadway, New York, NY 10019-6785.

Library of Congress Cataloging-in-Publication Data

Hourdebaigt, Jean-Pierre
    Canine massage : a practical guide / Jean-Pierre Hourdebaigt and Shari L. Seymour.
        p.   cm.
    ISBN 0-87605-340-1
    1. Dogs—Diseases—Alternative treatment.   2. Massage for animals.   I. Seymour, Shari L.
    II. Title.
    SF991.H596   1999
    636.7'0895822—dc21   98-46582
                            CIP

Manufactured in the United States of America

10 9 8 7 6 5 4 3 2 1

C·O·N·T·E·N·T·S

L·I·S·T O·F F·I·G·U·R·E·S

A·C·K·N·O·W·L·E·D·G·M·E·N·T·S

To all dogs, thank you for making us smile, for sharing with us your stories, needs and secrets, and for inspiring us to write this book.

To the dog lovers and dog owners, our gratitude for your years of participation in our seminars, for sharing your knowledge, for giving us your feedback, support and encouragement. Like your dog, you have been a source of inspiration to us.

For making this publication possible, we thank:

Jim Berry, D.V.M., for contributing to and verifying the medical content of this book.

Cindy Teevens, for her support over the years, and for her knowledge of and talent for desktop publishing.

Shannon and Montana, for their modeling talents, patience and their enduring sense of humor.

I·N·T·R·O·D·U·C·T·I·O·N

Small animal medicine has strongly benefited from the progress of modern medicine. The benefits of alternative medicines, such as massage therapy, physiotherapy, chiropractic, acupuncture and herbology, no longer need to be proven. Such therapies have become widely accepted and recognized by the traditional medical community.

It is surprising that massage therapy has not been used more widely with animals, especially because so many of their physiological problems are similar to those of humans and are already treated with similar drugs and therapies.

Massage therapy is easily learned, easily applied and costs very little. It is one of the oldest forms of therapy and has been used since ancient times.

Today, advances in sports therapies allow us to apply techniques more knowledgeably, to better assist our faithful canine companions. Sports massage therapy techniques have kept pace with the changing methods of training, playing a very important role as a preventative therapy as well as in recovery from injury. With this increased understanding, these techniques have led us to a much richer relationship with the dog and resulted in better caring for his needs.

A more holistic approach using alternative medicines is now preferred by many dog lovers, breeders and trainers. "Holistic" means that in order to create an environment for the maintenance or restoration of health, we must consider the animal in his totality—the sum of his physical and psychological traits—rather than treating each symptom separately. We must be observant and take into consideration all the various factors affecting both the internal and external environments of the dog. How we view this complex totality can affect the animal for good or ill. Any dysfunction of the musculoskeletal system requires that an overall assessment be made as to the causative factors. We know that the body will strive to heal, repair and maintain itself—if the right conditions are present. In order to help the healing capacity of the body, the dog's emotional stability, lifestyle, nutritional balance, exercise and hygiene programs, as well as structural soundness, are our responsibility. Massage therapy allows us to trigger the body's ability to help itself back to health.

If you don't correct the factors responsible for the problems you are treating (whether postural, occupational, habitual, emotional, or musculoskeletal in origin), the treatment of these symptoms is never of more than short-term value and chances are good that the symptoms may return!

Until the advent of the holistic health movement, massage as a form of therapy had been neglected in human health care in traditional Western medicine and almost totally ignored in animal health care. The massage touch has a very strong healing influence on the dog, and benefits animals (or people) of all ages and conditions. It is widely used to prevent and relieve stress, as well as to assist in recovery from injuries. Massage techniques safely affect the whole body by enhancing the circulatory, muscular and nervous systems and their interdependent functioning. Massage will relax your dog when he is excited, and give him strength and flexibility when he is tired. Over time, it also will help soften sharp character traits.

Massage therapy is the manipulation of the soft tissues of the body to achieve specific goals of drainage, relaxation, or stimulation, as well as the release of muscle-related problems such as trigger points and stress points. It contributes to the overall economy of the body and to its ability to function efficiently.

Massage increases the circulation of body fluids (blood and lymph), which results in increased oxygenation. Increased oxygenation, in turn, acts as a tonic for a better metabolism, leading to enhanced performance and shorter recuperation time, especially for older and convalescing animals.

Massage helps reduce the build-up of fibrous tissue adhesions that result from inflammation caused by trauma (strain, blows) or wounds. Adhesions may cause stiffness and soreness when a dog moves.

Massage greatly contributes to relaxing the nervous system and helping the psychophysiologic self-regulation factors between body and mind. After several relaxing massage experiences, nervous or aggressive dogs will calm down and reveal a softer, more trusting nature.

Massage's healing function speeds up recovery and therefore can be useful in solving a variety of problems from simple tiredness from over-play, lack of vitality, convalescence and old age, to sprains, spasms, arthritis, or recovery from surgery or broken bones.

Furthermore, the touching aspect of massage increases the emotional bond with the animal—especially the young dog—allowing him to relax and accept being handled. From very early in his life, a dog recognizes love and care from the touch and licks of his mother (a gentle form of massage). Owing to his inherent nature, the dog appears to need lots of love, attention and care from his owner—a factor that allows most dogs to love massage. Studies have shown that deprivation of affection is as damaging to the dog (or other animals, including humans) as being deprived of essential dietary nutrients.

Not all animals enjoy being touched, however. "Touch shyness" is an indication of problems or phobia. In that case, communication with your dog is of the utmost importance. You need to proceed gently with a calm voice, increasing your touch progressively, perhaps using a food reward eventually when your dog lets you touch him. Regular gentle massages will considerably lessen the phobia.

Massage is a terrific diagnostic tool. You will be able to feel and detect any abnormalities such as muscle tension or swollen areas much sooner than by sight or grooming. Massage will help you avoid possible complications that could be very costly to treat.

In this book, you will find everything you need and want to know about massage movements, pressures, rhythms, techniques and sequences. Different routines are specifically designed for different situations. You will also learn about the various areas of stress in a working animal and the potential stress sites.

In order for canine massage to be successful you must be able to be sympathetic to your dog's state of mind, to sense accurately what your hands are feeling, to have a knowledge of the structures worked on, and to understand the movement or technique being employed and how it effects the dog. Much practice is required. Learn to "see" with your hands and listen as your dog's body "tells its own story." This is the most efficient way to contribute to your dog's overall health and well being while making his world a better place.

1

THE DOG AND MASSAGE THERAPY

In preparation for massaging your dog, it is important not only to have knowledge of the dog's anatomy and physiology but also to know the massage techniques. To get the best results from your work you need to give your full attention to your dog. By being fully attentive you will be better able to feel the structures of the dog's body and assess his needs at the time of the massage. Put aside your personal concerns or worries so you can completely involve yourself in the work. Do not start when you are stressed, anxious, tired or fearful. Your feelings will be passed on to the animal through your touch, so be relaxed and have a positive attitude. In other words, the way you are is the way the dog will be. If your mind is not on your work, it will reduce the quality and effectiveness of the massage and your dog will be the first one to notice.

Consider the "ambiance" of the room where you will be giving your dog his massage. Perhaps dim the lights and play soft music. This preparation will help you make the transition and prepare you for the massage. Indeed, when you first begin you may feel a little hesitant about giving

a massage, but with practice you will quickly overcome this feeling. As long as you truly connect with your pet during the massage, he will feel cared for, and that is most important. Another consideration is that if you want to know how it feels to be massaged, contact a licensed therapist in your area and treat yourself to a full body massage (a Swedish massage if possible). You will be able to experience first-hand the various massage strokes that are taught in this book as well as the routines and techniques, the relaxation, the caring feeling, and the depth of work that massage can provide. Then you will better understand the effect you produce on your pet when you deliver a massage.

APPROACHING THE DOG

Your first contact, the actual first few minutes with the animal, is crucial for the positive development of the massage. Dogs, like humans, will suddenly tense up if they feel their bodies are being invaded. It is crucial you develop some trust between you and the dog you massage. We recommend that you observe the animal briefly before starting. If you approach a dog with an understanding of his nature and immediately make him feel secure, your dog will learn to trust you. Remember your dog needs to be "massage trained." Use carefully chosen positive reinforcement words (for example, relax, let go, etc.), and practice praising and rewarding your animal when he acts appropriately.

Speak softly and kindly to the dog as you approach him. Present your hands fully opened. Do not move your hands too fast. Give your dog time to acknowledge you before you start. The dog's response will be to bring his head toward you and nuzzle you; this is how a dog shakes your hand. Meanwhile, evaluate the breathing rhythm and adapt your breathing to the dog's. This action will allow you to observe whether his inner state is calm or restless.

Once the dog has acknowledged you, quietly bring your right hand—your natural, giving hand—to the nose and lightly massage the face (nose ridge, ears, back of the head). Keep talking and praising your dog, furthering your bonding with the softness of your voice. Gently bring your left hand to the dog's attention, then start touching the neck lightly, at the back of the head. If the animal does not like this, bring your hand down to the withers.

The first hand contact needs to be very warm, thoughtful and rich in feeling and vibration, so this contact will have a strong, positive impact on the dog. Be smooth. There is no need to rush. A few minutes is all that it takes to establish this

crucial first impression. Keep your voice gentle and praising as your dog accepts this first massage contact. Then proceed with your massage. The relaxation routine in chapter 9 is the best way to start any massage session, especially if it is the first time.

Maintain verbal contact with your pet—praising or commending as needed—as you progress in the sessions and look for feedback signs from your dog (see below). Memorize the four "Ts": temperature, texture, tension and tenderness (see chapter 6 for full discussion). Your fingertip perceptions are very important; ensure that you are mentally connected with them at all times. Note your observations and record them after the treatment. A record of your efforts will help you remember all the details from one massage to the next and therefore appreciate the progress made. A record is especially helpful if you have several dogs to massage (see chapter 13, Record Keeping). Think of your dog as a very picky, demanding client who is always checking on you. You want to give him the best massage possible.

YOUR DOG'S FEEDBACK SIGNS

Be aware of the feedback signs your pet gives you. Learn to recognize the sure signs of apprehension: raising or turning the head towards you, eyes widening and becoming intense, skin twitching or flinching, fidgeting, tensing up, moving away from the pressure, breathing short and hard, whimpering or short to long yelping sounds.

On the other hand, eyes half-closed, head down, ears to the side or heavy sighs are sure signs of relaxation and enjoyment. Monitor your dog's body language constantly and adjust your work accordingly.

Pain and discomfort feedback signs from your dog should always be regarded as a warning signal. Sudden jolts or tensing during the massage may indicate that the pressure you are applying is too strong, or that you have found a significant tender spot, or that your dog simply is afraid of what you are doing. Take time to reassure your dog with a soft voice and gentle rubbing.

Also, owing to his genetic inheritance, certain parts of the dog's body have special social or psychological associations. For example, when you start massaging your dog, he may roll on his back right away, presenting you his abdomen as a sign of submission and willingness to be

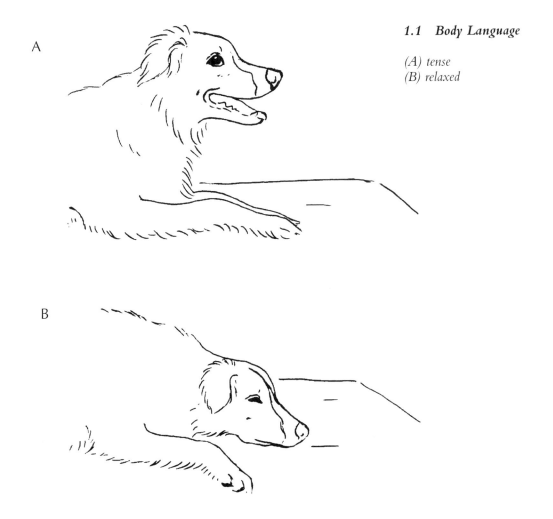

A

B

1.1 Body Language

(A) tense
(B) relaxed

massaged. Female dogs when in heat may raise their hind end and present it sexually when you start massaging the base of the tail. For the male dog, the groin or inguinal area is a very important body region. A dog presents his groin for contact as a sign of friendship or as a submissive gesture to dogs and people alike.

The neck area, the "scruff of the neck," is often a "shy spot" because of the grabbing and biting that is associated with dominance and fighting. Some male dogs may be agitated when you start working the neck area.

Also remember that intense restlessness, even 10 minutes into the massage, may indicate that the dog has a strong need to urinate. To avoid accidents, make sure you take your dog out before the massage.

THE DOG'S RESPONSE

Like humans, most dogs enjoy massage therapy when it is done with skilled hands. During their first massage experience, most dogs are very curious about what is happening to them and some may even display a defensive attitude. If he feels nervous or impatient, often a dog will move away. If this happens, do not hesitate to use firm commands to calm him, and when he obeys, praise him. Try to make this first experience fun and use lots of praise. Be patient about the results as well as with your dog.

Because dogs are social animals who strive to please their owners, they often respond well to a positive, reassuring voice, using lots of praise. Always talk to your dog in a calm, peaceful way when starting a massage. It will help to settle him down, especially during the first massage.

After a few sessions, most dogs will accept massage without any trouble and will enjoy it. Unfortunately, some dogs, because of improper handling (lack of training or bonding with humans during their early years) or traumatic histories (accidents, abuse), may be more fearful of massage, experiencing what we call "touch-shyness," which causes them to tense up all over. Time, patience, love and massage care will do wonders for this type of animal. Regular massage sessions (even if short) will definitely help this type of animal ease their fears, and relearn to trust, resulting in better behavior and handling. When dealing with an extreme case of phobia or restlessness, have your veterinarian check the animal. A mild tranquilizer for the first few massage sessions might be in order.

In some cases, touch-shyness in particular areas of the body (head, neck, paws or back) can indicate an underlying condition or sickness. Make sure that no contraindication applies (see page 9), and when in doubt check with your veterinarian before proceeding with the massage.

Take time to study the dog's temperament and character to make the proper connection during the first massage. Most dogs respond very positively to their first treatment. Puppies may engage in playful fighting with your hands during the massage. When dealing with a young dog, we recommend that you massage him after a good exercise or play workout so he will be tired and ready for some quiet massage time.

As a rule, use the relaxation routine from chapter 9 prior to giving any massage, at any time, to any dog. Don't rush! With each session you will build your dog's trust while allaying his instinctive fears.

As the dog relaxes during the session, his head will go down and his breathing will become deeper and slower with occasional sighing. To encourage the dog, praise him a lot when this occurs. Sighing is a definite indication of tension release. You will feel a strong energy field around the animal as he relaxes. Depending on the nature of the massage you use, the dog may either go to sleep or may perk up and be ready for exercise. Some dogs, like people, prefer a deeper and heavier or lighter and softer massage than others. You will be able to determine your animal's tolerance by starting slowly and gently to first trigger a relaxation response. Then, by gradually increasing your pressure and depth of work, you will be able to reach deep into the muscular and connective tissues without causing your dog to tense up or to try to get away from you. Indeed, if you use too heavy a pressure or manipulate the muscular tissue too hastily, your dog will let you know by tensing up or even yelping. Adjust your work accordingly and reassure your dog with lots of soft-spoken feedback.

POSITIONING THE DOG

When working on an average- or large-size dog, we recommend using a sturdy table with a blanket or large cushion on it. The proper height for the massage table should be measured in relation to your height. The measurement from the floor to your wrist should be equal to the height of the table with the blanket or cushion on it. A table at the correct height will help you to have good posture—back straight, shoulders and arms relaxed (see chapter 6)—and save on fatigue and muscle tension. A table that is either too high or too low will cause back and shoulder muscle tension to develop. To make the table accessible for your dog, use some kind of stairway, like a stool, a chair or a plastic crate for him to climb up on.

1.2   Correct Table Height

When working on a small dog, you can sit comfortably with your back straight and have a large pillow on your lap for your dog to lie on. Keep your back straight and arms relaxed. We will discuss this position in detail in chapter 6.

We do not recommend giving a massage to your dog while on the floor with you kneeling and bending over. This position will cause you lots of unnecessary discomfort and eventually pain, while in turn rendering your massage less efficient than if you were properly positioned and relaxed.

DURATION OF A MASSAGE

For your first massage—and especially if it is the animal's first massage—the relaxation massage routine (see chapter 9) is highly recommended. It should last between 5 to 8 minutes. Use your own judgment in relation to the dog's size, temperament and feedback signs. The first massage is a very special moment in which you should really emphasize a soft, mindful and caring contact to gain the animal's trust.

For the first full body massage, proceed gently and in a very relaxed manner, avoiding fast rhythm and deep pressure until the dog becomes confident in your work. This massage should last from 15 to 20 minutes, and up to 30 minutes for large dogs. After several sessions you can increase the time frame of your massages to 30 minutes. It is not unusual to spend 45 minutes on a thorough maintenance routine with a large dog accustomed to massage.

A maintenance massage routine (see chapter 9) can be done at any time to keep the animal's muscular structure fit; in the beginning it should last 15 or 20 minutes (in the early practice) and up to 30 minutes, depending on the dog's size.

A recuperation routine (see chapter 9) should be used after the dog has exercised in order to prevent stiffness or tying up; it should run from 10 to 15 minutes.

The dog's temperament plays an important role in his receptivity to massage. Most dogs will become restless, almost agitated, after massaging for 30 minutes, but some animals can easily take more than 30 minutes of a gentle, in-depth maintenance massage.

Your connection with the dog is important. When massaging a "stranger" for the first time, do not expect too much. But after several massage sessions, most dogs will love being massaged; they will lower their heads and go into relaxation mode very quickly. That's their way of showing you that they appreciate your work!

When dealing with an injury past the acute stage (first 24 hours), a massage should, depending on the symptoms, last from 10 to 20 minutes maximum. This includes hydrotherapy and stretching time if applicable. The severity of the injury and the degree of inflammation present in the tissues will dictate the nature of your massage. Always check with your veterinarian or massage therapist before you start. Chapter 8 presents several massage techniques that are commonly used for treating injuries. Always keep in mind that injured tissues are painful and that you must avoid overworking them. Keep your massage short in the beginning. As the inflammation decreases, you can proportionally increase the duration of your massage sessions.

When working on a specific area (for example, a large area such as the hindquarters or the back), you should not spend more than 5 to 10 minutes on that part, otherwise you risk overworking the structures. Such overwork could result in inflammation and irritation of the tissues. For the same reason, do not spend more than 5 minutes on a small area such as the upper neck or the stifle. Judge the situation carefully. Consider the state of the tissues and the dog's tolerance at the time of massage. And always relieve the inflammation by following the massage with lots of drainage (see page 113) and cold hydrotherapy (see page 72).

Evaluate and plan your treatment mentally before you start, and keep track of time as you move around the body. With practice, this technique will become second nature to you.

WHEN TO MASSAGE YOUR DOG

Depending on your goals and the situation at hand, you need to find the most suitable time in order to achieve the best results. Basically, any time is a good time to massage your dog, but you want to choose the moment when your dog will be most receptive.

The most effective use of massage therapy is to integrate the massage into your everyday routine of working with your animal. For example, you can massage right after grooming, after exercise, or when putting your dog away for the night. You can choose a morning or evening schedule for a thorough, full-body session. You are the judge and common sense is the rule.

In any case, always observe the following guidelines:

❖ Always perform a health check to ensure that there are no contraindications prevailing prior to massaging the animal (see later in this chapter).

❖ Develop a routine and base your work on it. A repetitive pattern ensures confidence and relaxation (see chapter 9).

When you want to deliver a good massage to your animal, it is best to wait for the dog's moment. Evaluating your dog's temperament will help you discover his best time. If yours is a morning dog, work in the morning. If an afternoon dog, work in the afternoon. If a night dog, work in the late evening. Once your dog has experienced the magic of your hands, he will often come up to you, and lean against you to beg for a rub, moving around so that you massage just where he wants you to.

The training and lifestyle your dog is used to also will play a role in determining a good time for a massage. Here are a few examples of different massage routines and a dog's activity: a maintenance massage before exercise; a recuperation routine after exercise; a relaxation massage before bedtime, after a long day, before and after traveling, or when restless or in pain. Also, keep in mind that outside influences can affect your dog, construction in the house, visitors, arrival of a new dog or other pet, an approaching electrical storm, strong winds, and so on. A dog may also be restless because of extremely hot weather, a heavy training schedule with rich food, and during competition, traveling, and feeding time.

Remember, the relaxation routine (see chapter 9) can be done at any time. It is always used to start a full body massage. The relaxation routine works wonders in switching a dog's mood, especially if it is depressed, naughty, mischievous or simply tense.

The maintenance routine is best done when the dog is warm following some exercise (walk, play) either morning or evening. If the dog cannot be warmed up by exercise, cover him with a blanket or use a hot water bottle to increase circulation.

The warm-up routine (see chapter 9) is always done before heavy training to prevent possible muscle tear.

The recuperation routine (see chapter 9) is always done after heavy playing or training to help the dog recover faster by eliminating toxins in a matter of a few hours.

Massage after injury should be worked into a schedule followed by stretching exercises, or a rest period, depending on the symptoms during recovery. Remember to work with your veterinarian to ensure maximum benefit to your dog.

DO'S AND DON'TS

The ambiance in which you work will directly influence the efficiency of the massage. Here are some guidelines for you to observe in order to ensure maximum safety for both you and the dog when giving a massage treatment.

DO'S:

✔ Do check with your veterinarian if you suspect your dog is not feeling well.

✔ Do maintain a soothing atmosphere: not too much traffic, not too many noises. Eventually you may play peaceful, quiet music.

✔ Do keep other pets away.

✔ Do work indoors.

✔ Do use a massage table cushioned with a blanket or large pillow. Keep the area around the table free of obstacles.

✔ Do allow the dog complete freedom of head movement because this allows for better relaxation and for more feed-back signals to you.

✔ Do wait after strenuous exercise.

✔ Do wait two hours after eating.

✔ Do check your dog and remove burrs, mud, etc. before you begin a massage.

✔ Do always start massaging with a very light pressure and progress to deeper work.

✔ Do keep your fingernails short and avoid wearing jewelry and heavy perfume.

✔ Do keep talking to the animal throughout the treatment.

✔ Do always pay attention to the feedback signs (eyes, ears, tail, breathing, noises and change in posture).

✔ Do keep records of your observations and the types of treatment you give.

✔ Do establish a treatment and exercise schedule for the following weeks, or until recovery if the dog is injured.

✔ Do wear loose-fitting clothing to give yourself freedom of movement.

DON'TS:

✗ Don't disregard the physiological signs of contraindications.

✗ Don't allow loud music, commotion, or smoking.

✗ Don't allow other pets to wander around. Prevent such an intrusion before starting the treatment.

✗ Don't work in a narrow space.

✗ Don't work on a dirty dog—one with mud or burrs on his body.

✗ Don't work hastily, too quickly or too forcefully.

✗ Don't have long fingernails or wear jewelry.

✗ Don't stop verbal feedback to the dog—he needs praise and reassurance.

✗ Don't talk loudly or shout.

✗ Don't talk to somebody else while working. You will lose your concentration and this will affect the quality of your work. The dog will definitely feel the difference.

✗ Don't use heavy pressure at the start.

✗ Don't ignore feedback signs from the dog (eyes, ears, tail, breathing, noises).

✗ Don't work right after the dog has completed heavy exercise or has eaten.

✗ Don't be angry or in a bad mood when working on a dog.

✗ Don't think negatively.

CONTRAINDICATIONS TO MASSAGING A DOG

Contraindications refer to the specific situations in which you should not massage a dog. If these conditions exist, consult your veterinarian. For example:

❖ Do not massage a dog with a temperature over 104°F or 39.5°C. A dog's regular temperature is 101°F or 38.5°C. An increase in temperature occurs during serious illnesses; usually a sick dog is depressed, off his feed, and doesn't want to move. Feverish conditions necessitate complete rest. Massage will only worsen the situation by increasing an already accelerated blood circulation. Check with your vet. The laying on of hands over the head and over the sacrum will soothe the dog.

❖ When your dog is suffering from shock.

❖ When there is an open (broken skin) or healing (bleeding) wound, avoid that particular area. You may massage the rest of the body to release compensatory tension or excess swelling.

❖ When there is acute trauma such as a torn muscle, or an area with internal bleeding such as an acute hematoma following a strong blow, use ice for the first few hours. Massage can resume in the chronic stage (after 72 hours).

❖ When there is an acute sprain, use ice until the initial swelling goes down, then use the swelling technique from chapter 8.

❖ When there are severe forms of functional nervous diseases such as distemper, for example, the nerve stimulation would make the dog extremely uncomfortable.

❖ When there are acute nerve problems or nerve irritation (neuralgia) in a particular area following a wound or a bad stretch, the laying on of hands may soothe. Use cold hydrotherapy to numb the nerve endings before and after the laying on of hands.

❖ During colitis, diarrhea, pregnancy or hernias, use just a light stroking on the abdomen and only if the dog does not mind.

❖ Acute rheumatism and acute arthritis are too painful to permit massage. Massage would worsen the inflammation. Instead, use cold hydrotherapy locally. Once the acute stage is relieved, resume your massage. Chronic stages of rheumatism and arthritis require different massage treatment. Light massage over the areas affected will relax the

compensatory tension from the muscles supporting those structures. Do not work deeply around the joints.

❖ Calcium deposits around joints or within soft tissues should not be massaged as it could result in increased inflammation in these areas. Check with your veterinarian for possible surgical removal.

❖ Inflammatory conditions such as phlebitis would be worsened by direct massage. Use cold hydrotherapy and check with your veterinarian.

❖ Tumors and cysts of cancerous origin are contraindicated; massage will spread them. Avoid the affected areas, but you may massage the rest of the body. Check with your vet.

Massage is formally contraindicated in the following conditions, because massage would contribute to spreading the problem:

❖ Skin problems of fungal origin such as ringworm, infectious conditions, pneumonia and bacterial skin disease.

❖ Acute stages of viral diseases such as parainfluenza or distemper.

Be careful when dealing with what appears to be an abnormal situation. When in doubt, contact a veterinarian. When massage is contraindicated, it is best to keep your dog warm, properly hydrated and undisturbed. Follow your veterinarian's advice about medication. The laying of hands (see chapter 7) will often sooth an irritated area. Hydrotherapy (see chapter 5) also will relieve the inflammation and pain considerably, assisting recovery and definitively comforting your animal.

Knowing how to safely approach an animal for massage is part of the secret to a successful massage. Your patience, perseverance, good humor, kindness, knowledge and skills will reduce the psychological and physical barrier between the dog and you, leading to better communication with the animal.

2

Knowing some of the anatomy and physiology of your dog will help you develop a better ability to "feel-see" when massaging your pet, as well as sharpen your massage skills. This chapter describes the various systems of the dog. Detailed information concerning each individual system is beyond the scope of this book. However, since massage mostly deals with the musculoskeletal system, which induces body movement, the nervous system, the skeletal system and the muscular system, all will be described in greater detail to further your understanding.

The nine principal systems of the dog's body are:

1. nervous
2. skeletal
3. muscular
4. circulatory
5. respiratory
6. digestive
7. urinary
8. endocrine
9. reproductive

The dog's health depends on the harmonious working relationship of all these body systems.

THE NERVOUS SYSTEM

The nervous system (the brain, spinal cord, sensory and motor nerves) controls the workings of all other systems. The nervous system integrates and controls every body function, both voluntary and involuntary; it processes all information and governs all commands to the body. Within the nervous system are found:

❖ The central nervous system (CNS). The CNS is made up of the brain and spinal cord, which perform very specific functions. Massage does not directly affect the CNS, only indirectly via the peripheral nervous system (PNS).

❖ The peripheral nervous system (PNS). The PNS conveys nerve

2.1 Points of the Dog

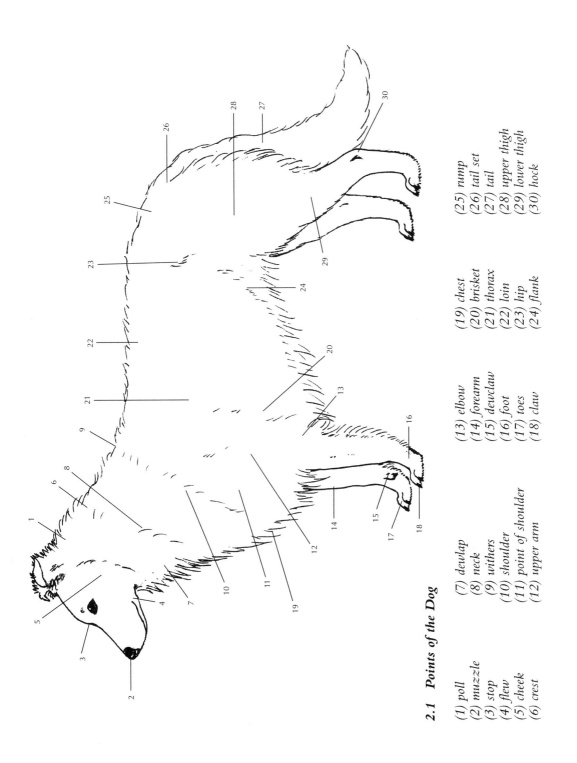

(1) poll
(2) muzzle
(3) stop
(4) flew
(5) cheek
(6) crest

(7) dewlap
(8) neck
(9) withers
(10) shoulder
(11) point of shoulder
(12) upper arm

(13) elbow
(14) forearm
(15) dewclaw
(16) foot
(17) toes
(18) claw

(19) chest
(20) brisket
(21) thorax
(22) loin
(23) hip
(24) flank

(25) rump
(26) tail set
(27) tail
(28) upper thigh
(29) lower thigh
(30) hock

impulses through the efferent or motor nerves (which carry information from the CNS to the body parts), and the afferent or sensory nerves (which carry information from the body parts to the CNS). These nerves exit the spinal column at the vertebrae (spinal bones). Massage directly influences the PNS (pressure and rhythm).

The PNS's nerve tissues are composed of many filaments that are very susceptible to pressure. In the case of a strong trauma, when significant or severe pressure is applied to a nerve, nerve impulses can stop traveling along it. As a consequence, two things can happen: the loss of sensation or feedback due to the loss of sensory nerve impulses from the body part to the CNS and the degeneration and eventual shrinking of the tissue in the immediate area of the affected nerve as a result of lost motor nerve impulses from the CNS to the body part.

The overall functioning of the nervous system is ensured by the autonomic nervous system (ANS), which maintains a stable internal environment. The ANS governs the vital organs and their complex functions that are normally carried out involuntarily, such as breathing, circulation, digestion, elimination and the immune response. The ANS also helps coordinate the locomotor function for safety and smoothness of movements of the body during action.

The autonomic nervous system has two major divisions: the sympathetic and the parasympathetic. Both originate in the brain.

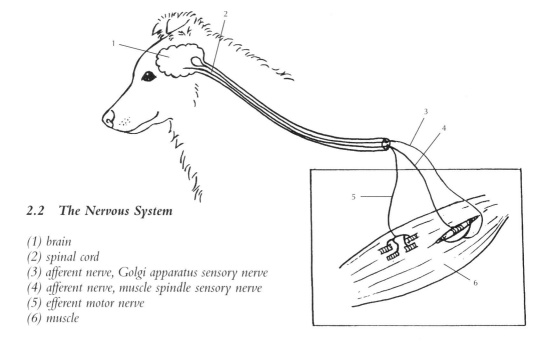

2.2   The Nervous System

(1) brain
(2) spinal cord
(3) afferent nerve, Golgi apparatus sensory nerve
(4) afferent nerve, muscle spindle sensory nerve
(5) efferent motor nerve
(6) muscle

The sympathetic division causes the body to respond to danger, adversity, stress, anger and ecstasy by increasing the heart rate, blood pressure, the volume of air exchange and the volume of blood flowing to the muscles—all of which are needed for the dog to spring into action. The sympathetic division is often described as the "fight or flight" division. Many massage routines (see chapter 9) or techniques (see chapter 8) will cause a general stimulation of the sympathetic division resulting in mobilization of resources to prepare the body to act or to deal with emergencies.

The parasympathetic division monitors body functions during times of sickness (when dog is feverish), rest, sleep, digestion and elimination when the body is not ready to spring into action. A general stimulation of the parasympathetic seems to promote relaxation and the vegetative functions of the body such as breathing, circulation, digestion, immune response and reproduction. The relaxation massage routine in chapter 9 is designed to relax the nervous system.

THE SKELETAL SYSTEM

The skeletal system serves as a framework for the dog's body, giving the muscles something to work against and defining the animal's overall size and shape. The skeleton also protects the dog's vital internal tissues and organs: for example, the skull protects the brain; the rib cage protects the lungs and heart; the vertebral column protects the spinal cord.

BONES

Bones come in different shapes and sizes and have specific functions. With the exception of the teeth, which are enamel covered, bones are the body's hardest tissues. They are made up of minerals (mostly calcium). Bones are capable of withstanding great compression, torque and tension. Bones are covered and protected by a tough membrane, a layer of connective tissue called the periosteum. The periosteum provides for the attachment of the joint capsules, the ligaments and the tendons. Injury to the periosteum may result in undesirable bone growths. Bones are held together by ligaments; muscles are attached to the bones by tendons. The articulating surface of the bone is covered with a thick, smooth cartilage that diminishes concussion and friction.

There are long bones (in the limbs), short bones (in the wrist, knee and hock), flat bones (rib cage, skull and shoulder blade) and irregular bones (vertebrae of the spine, sacrum, and tail, as well as some bones of the skull).

Long bones function mainly as levers and aid in the support of weight. For example, the foreleg includes the humerus, radius and ulna, and the hind leg includes the femur, tibia and fibula.

Short bones, such as the carpus (wrist) and tarsus (hock), are found in complex joints and absorb concussion.

Flat bones protect and enclose the cavities containing vital organs, for example, the skull (brain) and ribs (heart and lungs).

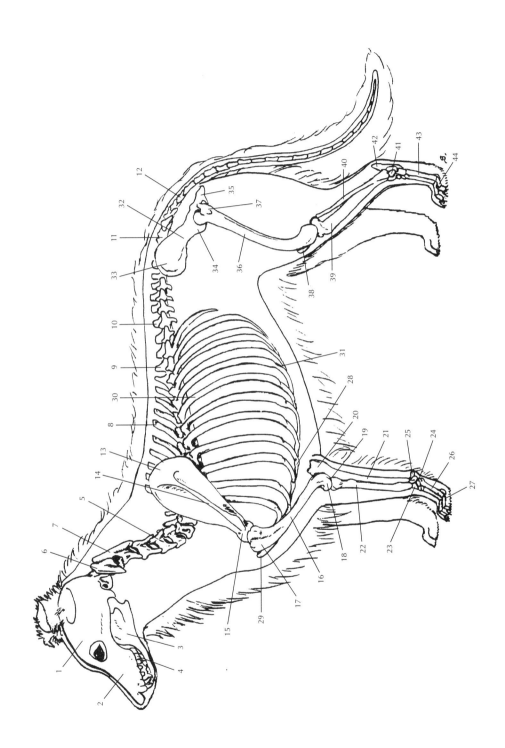

2.3   Skeleton of the Dog

(1) cranium
(2) mandible
(3) lower jaw
(4) teeth
(5) cervical vertebrae—7
(6) atlas (first cervical vertebra)
(7) axis (second cervical vertebra)
(8) thoracic vertebrae—13
(9) last thoracic vertebra
(10) lumbar vertebrae—7
(11) sacrum (3 fused vertebrae)
(12) coccygeal vertebrae (usually 18)
(13) scapula
(14) scapular spine (bone ridge)
(15) neck of scapula
(16) humerus
(17) head of humerus
(18) lateral condyle of humerus
(19) elbow joint
(20) olecranon process of the ulna (point of elbow)
(21) ulna
(22) radius

(23) wrist joint
(24) carpus bones
(25) pisiforme bone
(26) metacarpus bone
(27) phalanges
(28) sternum (breastbone)
(29) manubrium sternum
(30) rib
(31) costal cartilage
(32) pelvis
(33) ilium
(34) pubis
(35) ischium
(36) femur
(37) trochanter major
(38) patella (knee)
(39) tibia
(40) fibula
(41) tarsus bones
(42) tuber calcanei
(43) metatarsus
(44) phalangis pedis

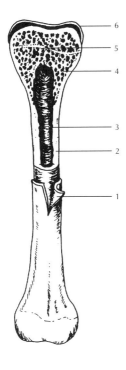

2.4   Parts of a Bone

(1) periosteum
(2) compact bone
(3) medullary cavity
(4) spongy bone with marrow cavities
(5) epiphyseal plate
(6) articulate hyaline cartilage

Flat bones also provide large areas for the attachment of muscles, for example, the shoulder blades and hips. Both long and flat bones have a central cavity that produces special cells. Marrow and osteoclast cells form in the cavity of long bones, while red blood cells develop in the cavity of flat bones.

So-called irregular bones have many bony projections of various shapes and sizes that offer attachments for muscles, tendons and ligaments. For example, vertebrae are irregular bones in the spinal column that provide solid anchoring for locomotor muscle groups.

The skeleton is made up of:

❖ The skull and its facial bones (nasal, frontal, parietal and jaw bones).

❖ The spine, with its 7 cervical, 13 thoracic, 7 lumbar and 3 fused sacral vertebrae. The tail is usually made up of 18 to 23 caudal vertebrae, although this number can vary considerably.

❖ The rib cage, made up of 13 pairs of ribs springing from the thoracic vertebrae, curving forward and meeting at the sternum (breastbone).

❖ The forelegs, which carry 60 percent of the dog's body weight. The foreleg comprises the scapula (shoulder blade); humerus, radius and ulna; the carpus bones (wrist), which is made up of eight carpal bones arranged in two rows: the metacarpal and phalanges.

❖ The hind legs, which comprise the pelvis (ilium, ischium and pubis); femur, tibia and fibula; the hock (comprising seven tarsal bones); and the metatarsus and phalanges pedis bones.

JOINTS

The joint permits certain parts of the bony frame to articulate and produce motion. Joints are the meeting places between two bones. Movement of the dog is dependent upon the contraction of muscles and the corresponding articulation of the joints.

Some joints are not movable and are referred to as fibrous or cartilaginous joints because they lack a joint cavity.

Immovable joints include those of the sacroiliac and the skull.

But most joints in the body are movable. They are called synovial joints and include the shoulder, elbow, wrist, knee and hock, all of which permit a great range of motion. The ends of the bones are lined with hyaline cartilage, which provides a smooth surface between the bones and acts as a shock-absorber during times of compression (when jumping or during quick turns). Joints are surrounded by joint capsules, also known as the capsular ligaments. The inner layer of the capsular wall is made up of a delicate layer of synovial membrane, which produces a viscous, lubricating secretion known as the synovial fluid.

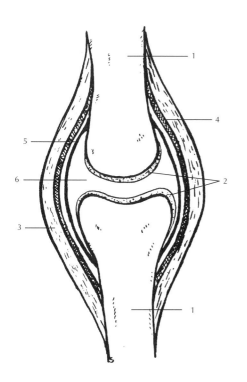

2.5   Parts of a Joint

(1) bone
(2) hyaline cartilage
(3) ligament
(4) fibrous capsule
(5) synovial lining
(6) joint cavity (with synovial fluid)

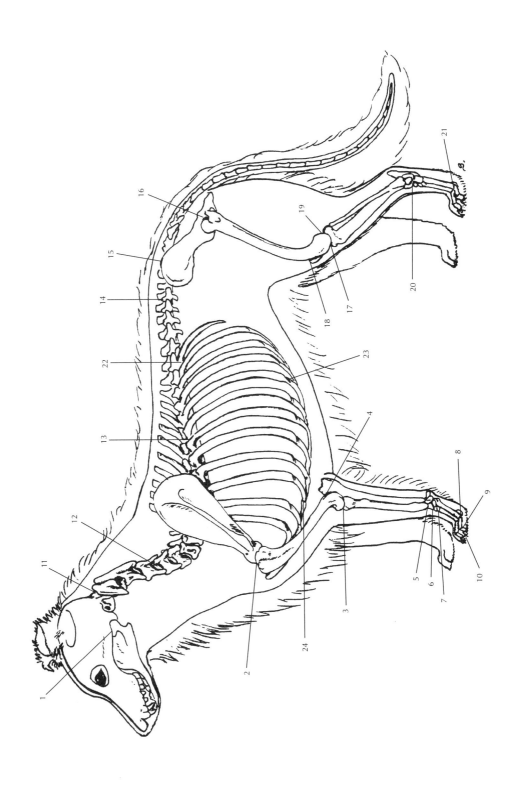

2.6 Joints of the Dog

(1) jaw
(2) shoulder
(3) elbow, humeroradial component
(4) elbow, humeroulnar component
(5) wrist
(6) intercarpal
(7) carpometacarpal
(8) metacarpophalangeal
(9) proximal interphalangeal
(10) distal interphalangeal
(11) atlantooccipital
(12) cervical intervertebral

(13) thoracic intervertebral
(14) lumbosacral
(15) sacroiliac
(16) hip
(17) knee (stifle)
(18) femoropatellar component of knee
(19) femorotibial component of knee
(20) ankle (hock)
(21) metatarsophalangeal
(22) costovertebral
(23) costochondral
(24) costosternal

The joint can perform many movements, including flexion (bending), extension, abduction (drawing away from the middle of the body), adduction (drawing back to the center) and rotation.

LIGAMENTS

A ligament is a band of tissue that connects one bone to another (tendons connect muscles to bones). Ligaments are made up of collagen, a fibrous protein found in the connective tissue. Ligaments have a limited blood supply and because of this injuries or sprains take longer to heal in a ligament than in a muscle.

Most ligaments are located around joints to give extra support (capsular ligaments and collateral ligaments), to prevent excessive or abnormal ranges of motion and to resist the pressure of lateral torque (a twisting motion).

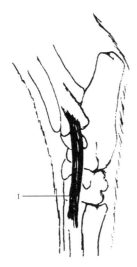

2.7 A Ligament

(1) lateral collateral ligament of tarsal joint

Ligaments are very tough yet have little contraction power. Therefore they must work in conjunction with muscles. Within very narrow limits, ligaments are somewhat elastic. From human sport medicine we know that if a ligament is overstretched or repeatedly stretched, it might lose up to 25 percent of its strength; such a ligament may need surgical stitching to recover its full tensile strength. Severe ligament sprain will lead to joint instability.

Several ligamentous structures help support and protect the vertebral column, pelvis, neck and limbs from suddenly imposed strain.

THE MUSCULAR SYSTEM

The muscular system provides the power and means to move the bony frame. There are three classes of muscle: smooth, cardiac and skeletal. The smooth and cardiac muscles are involuntary, or autonomic; they play a part in the digestive, respiratory, circulatory and urogenital systems. For the most part, the skeletal muscle is voluntary; it functions in the dog's movements. In massage, we are concerned with the more than 700 skeletal muscles that are responsible for movement in the dog.

There are at least two main types of muscle fiber: slow-twitch fibers (ST) and fast-twitch fibers (FT).

ST fibers are aerobic fibers and need oxygen to do their job. Thus ST fibers require a good supply of blood to bring oxygen to them and to remove waste products created during exercise. ST fibers also have strong endurance qualities.

FT fibers are anaerobic fibers; they do not need oxygen to work and therefore are able to deliver the quick muscular effort required for a sudden burst of speed. However, FT fibers are only able to perform for short periods of time.

The ratio of ST to FT fibers is genetically inherited. Careful selective breeding can emphasize these features in a dog.

Regardless of the FT/ST fiber ratio, a muscle is made up of a fleshy part and two tendon attachments. The muscle belly, or fleshy part, is the part that contracts in response to a nervous command. During contraction, the muscle fibers basically fold on themselves, which shortens them and results in muscle movement. The muscle belly is made up of many muscle fibers arranged in bundles with each bundle wrapped in connective tissue (fascia). The fascia covers, supports and separates each individual muscle bundle and the whole muscle itself. This arrangement allows for greater support, strength and flexibility in the movement between each of the muscle groups.

TENDONS

The tendon is the muscle part that attaches to the bone. The tendon is made up of connective tissue—a dense, white fibrous tissue much like that of a ligament. The origin tendon is the tendon that attaches the muscle to the least movable bone; the insertion tendon is the tendon that attaches the muscle to the

movable bone, so that on contraction the insertion is brought closer to the origin. Tendons attach to the periosteum of the bone; the fibers of the tendon blend with the periosteum fibers because of their similar collagen make-up. Tendons can be fairly short or quite long as with some of the flexor and extensor muscles of the lower legs. Usually, tendons are rounded, but they can be flattened like the tendons that attach along the spine. Because of their high-tensile strength, tendons can endure an enormous amount of tension, usually more than the muscle itself can produce; consequently, tendons do not rupture easily. They are not as elastic as muscle fibers, but they are more elastic than ligament fibers.

Tendons can "stress up" after heavy exercise, meaning that they can stay contracted. Gentle massage and stretching will loosen residual tension (see the origin-insertion technique in chapter 8).

Inflamed tendons are at great risk of being strained or overstretched. Many leg muscles have long tendons that run down the legs over the joints. These tendons are protected by sheaths, or tendon bursae. Chronic irritation of the sheath can result in excess fluid production and soft swellings. Massage and cold hydrotherapy (see chapter 5) will help circulation and keep inflammation down. If the inflammation persists, check with your veterinarian.

SKELETAL MUSCLES

Muscles come in all shapes and sizes. Some are small and some large, some are

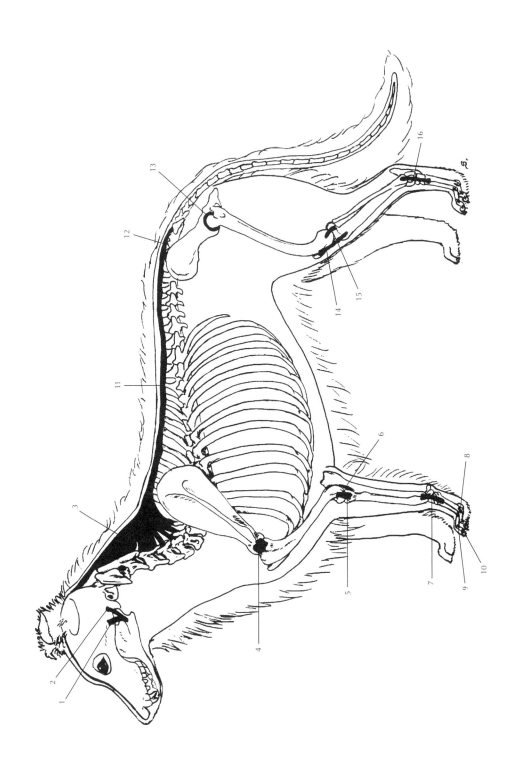

2.8 Ligaments of the Dog

(1) lateral ligament of jaw joint
(2) caudal (posterior) ligament of jaw joint
(3) nuchal ligament
(4) capsular ligament of shoulder joint
(5) lateral collateral ligament of elbow joint
(6) lateral transverse radioulnar ligament
(7) lateral collateral ligament of carpal joint
(8) lateral collateral ligament of metacarpophalangeal joint

(9) collateral ligament of proximal interphalangeal joint
(10) collateral ligament of distal interphalangeal joint
(11) supraspinous ligament
(12) dorsal sacroiliac ligament
(13) capsular ligament of hip joint
(14) lateral patellar ligament
(15) lateral collateral ligament of knee (stifle) joint
(16) lateral collateral ligament of tarsal joint

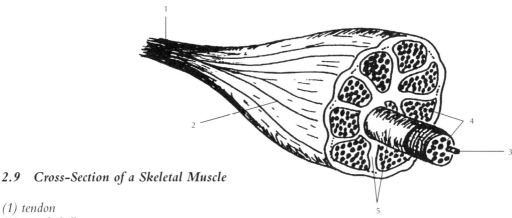

2.9   Cross-Section of a Skeletal Muscle

(1) tendon
(2) muscle belly
(3) muscle fiber (containing thick and thin filaments)
(4) bundles (made up of fibers)
(5) fascia

thin and some are bulky. Look at the muscle charts to note the variety of shapes in the dog's muscle structure.

Muscles act together to give the dog its grace and power. Muscles work in three different ways: isometric contraction, concentric contraction and eccentric contraction.

Isometric contraction occurs when a muscle contracts without causing any movement. During standing, for example, isometric contraction ensures stability.

Concentric contraction occurs when a muscle shortens as it contracts, causing articular movements. Concentric contraction is mostly seen in regular movements such as protraction (forward movement) or retraction (backward movement) of the limbs and in any movement of the neck or back.

Eccentric contraction occurs when a muscle gradually releases as it elongates. Eccentric contraction assists regular movements by avoiding jerky unstable actions; it also plays a role in shock

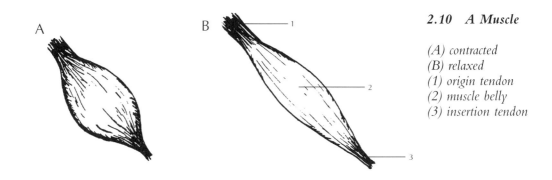

2.10   A Muscle

(A) contracted
(B) relaxed
(1) origin tendon
(2) muscle belly
(3) insertion tendon

absorption during the landing phase of jumping.

Skeletal muscles are highly elastic and have strong contractile power. They respond to motor nerve impulses and as a result, the contraction mechanism is a generated process. The release process is not a generated process, but rather is a natural relaxation of the muscle as a result of the cessation of the motor nerve impulses that originally "asked" the muscle to contract.

Muscles are equipped with two types of sensory nerve endings: the Golgi apparatus and the muscle spindle.

The Golgi apparatus nerve endings send feedback impulses to the brain as to the whereabouts of the muscle; this process is referred to as proprioception. The Golgi nerve endings are mostly located where the muscle and the tendons come together.

The muscle spindle nerve endings prevent overstretching of the muscle fibers. As its name implies, this nerve fiber coils around the length of the muscle bundle. Reaching a given length, the muscle spindle fires nerve impulses that trigger a fast reflex motor nerve reaction to induce immediate contraction of the muscle fibers. Thus the overstretching and potential tearing of fibers is prevented. This is a safety reflex mechanism.

When a muscle develops a contracture, the muscle fibers stay contracted. This could result in a spasm. With a contracture the natural relaxation process will not happen but pain and motion problems (restriction) will.

When a muscle overstretches, a spasm often results. A spasm is a tetanic (violent) contraction of a muscle in response to overstretching or trauma, whereby the muscle is unable to release its rigidity. A microspasm, or stress point, however, is a small spasm occurring in just a few fibers of the muscle bundle. Microspasms have a cumulative effect over a period of time and result in a full spasm.

Sometimes a muscle is stretched past its limits and muscle fibers will tear. This causes an immediate muscle spasm and triggers an inflammation response with swelling at the site of injury. As part of the healing process, new connective tissue is laid down in an irregular scattered pattern within the muscle fiber arrangement. Unfortunately this scar tissue reduces the muscle tensile strength, flexibility and elasticity. Massage therapy can reduce the amount of scar tissue by applying kneadings and frictions after proper warmup of the tissues. Also, stretching is a great technique for preventing and reducing the formation of scar tissue.

A heavily exercised muscle will often develop a light inflammation within its fibers. This is a normal process that promotes formation of new muscle fibers. It is often seen during early phases of training or in growing dogs. It is important to keep any inflammation under control in order to avoid the formation of scar tissue. To keep the inflammation down, use cold hydrotherapy (see chapter 5), and deep massage (see chapter 7, friction movements). These techniques will stimulate circulation, bringing new oxygen and nutrients to promote healing, and break down scar tissue within the muscle fibers.

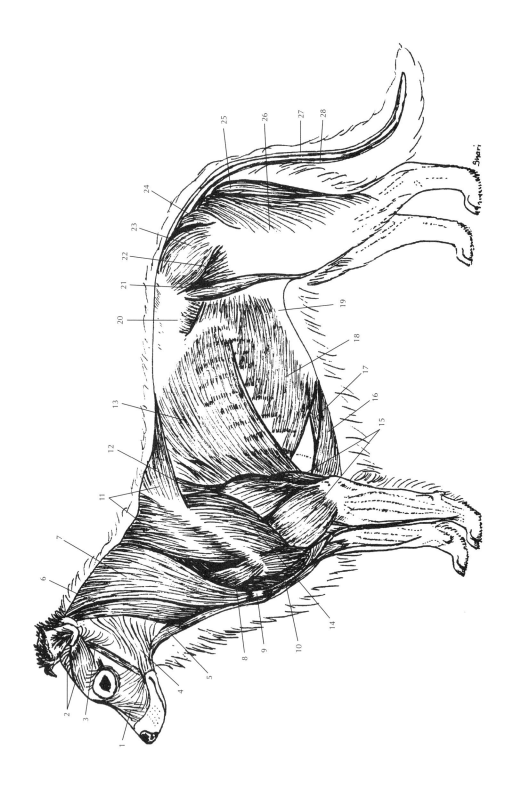

2.11 Muscles of the Dog, Superficial Layer

(1) levator nasolabialis muscle
(2) common muscle of the ears
(3) zygomaticus muscle
(4) cervical subcutaneous muscle
(5) strenohyoidei muscle
(6) sternomastoid muscle
(7) brachiocephalicus section of cledomastoid muscle
(8) levator scapula muscle
(9) tendinous band
(10) mastoid muscle
(11) trapezius anterior and posterior muscles
(12) infraspinatus muscle
(13) latissimus dorsi muscle
(14) deltoid muscle

(15) triceps brachii muscle (long & short head)
(16) pectoralis minor profondus muscle
(17) rectus abdominus muscle
(18) abdominal external oblique muscle
(19) aponeurosis
(20) abdominal internal oblique muscle
(21) sartorius muscle
(22) tensor fascia latae muscle
(23) gluteus medius muscle
(24) gluteus maximus superficialis muscle
(25) semitendinosus muscle
(26) biceps femoris muscle
(27) levator muscle of the tail
(28) abductor muscle of the tail

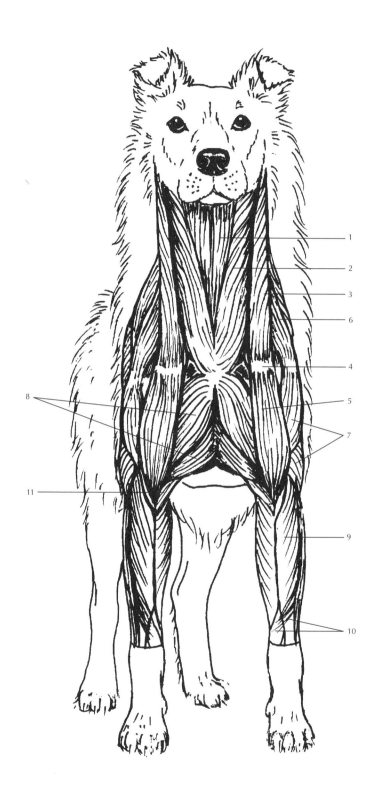

2.12 Muscles of the Dog, Anterior (Front) View

(1) sternohyoidei
(2) sternomastoid
(3) brachiocephalicus section of the cledomastoid muscle
(4) tendinous band
(5) mastoid muscle
(6) levator scapula
(7) deltoid muscle
(8) pectoralis major superficialis muscle
(9) extensor carpi radialis muscle
(10) abductor pollicis longus muscle
(11) biceps brachii muscle

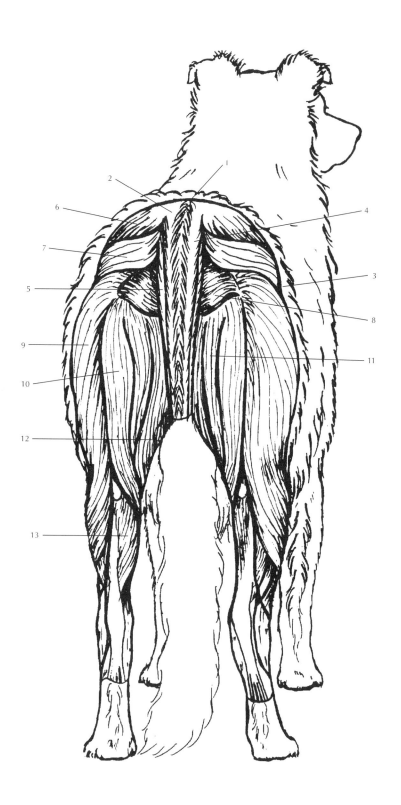

2.13 Muscles of the Dog, Posterior (Rear) View

(1) point of croup
(2) dock of tail
(3) point of hip or haunch (tuber coxae)
(4) levator muscles of tail
(5) depressor muscles of tail
(6) gluteus medius muscle
(7) gluteus maximus muscle
(8) obturator internus muscle
(9) biceps femoris muscle
(10) semitendinosus muscle
(11) semimembranosus muscle
(12) gracilis muscle
(13) gastrocnemius muscle

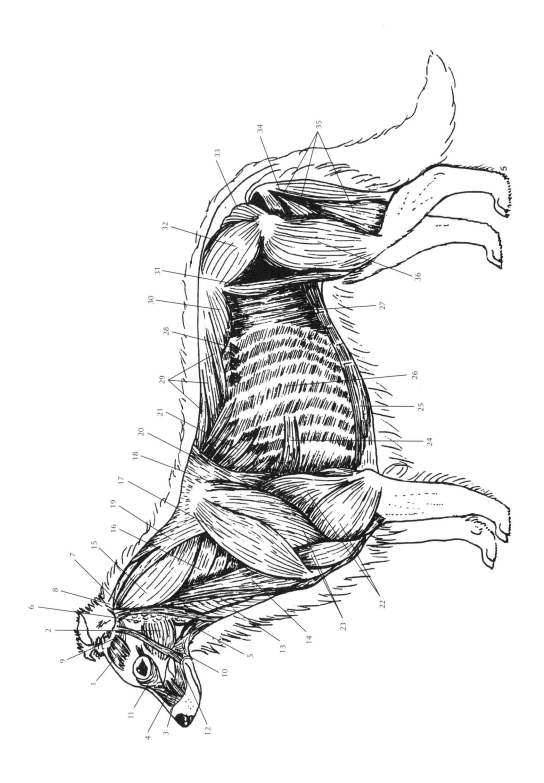

2.14 Muscles of the Dog, Deeper Layer

(1) temporalis muscle
(2) masseter muscle
(3) nasal muscle
(4) buccalis muscle
(5) glandula parotis
(6) glandula subnaxillaris
(7) depressor auri muscle
(8) occipitalis muscle
(9) exterior adductor muscle of the ear
(10) digastric muscle
(11) orbicularis palpebrarum
(12) orbicularis oris muscle
(13) mastoid muscle
(14) levator scapula muscle
(15) splenius muscle
(16) serratus cervicis muscle
(17) supraspinatus muscle
(18) infraspinatus muscle

(19) rhomboid muscle
(20) teres major muscle
(21) serratus thoracis muscle
(22) triceps brachii muscle (long and short head)
(23) deltoid muscle
(24) scalenus muscle (part of)
(25) rectus abdominus muscle
(26) intercostal muscle
(27) transverse abdominal muscle
(28) serratus posterior muscle
(29) longissimus dorsi muscle
(30) iliocostalis muscle
(31) sartorius muscle
(32) gluteus medius muscle
(33) gluteus maximus superficialis muscle
(34) semimembranosus muscle
(35) semitendinosus muscle
(36) quadriceps femoris muscle

As a result of heavy exercise, a stress point may develop close to the origin tendon of the muscle. A stress point is a small spasm in the muscle fiber. Keep your dog free of stress points by using the stress point technique in chapter 8.

Another side effect of an intense training and exercise program is the formation of trigger points. A trigger point is a combination of lactic acid build-up and motor nerve ending irritation mostly found in the fleshy part (belly) of the muscle.

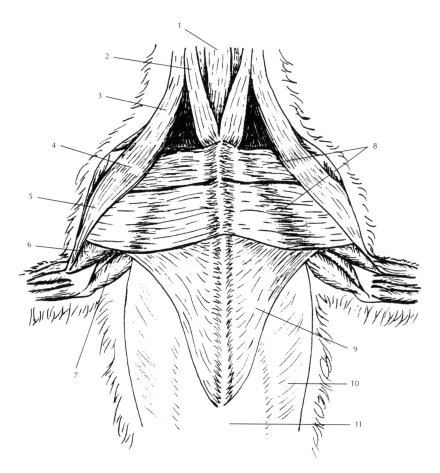

2.15 *Muscles of the Dog, Ventral (Lower) View*

(1) sternohyoidei muscle
(2) sternomastoid muscle
(3) brachiocephalicus section of cledomastoid muscle
(4) tendinous band
(5) mastoid muscle
(6) biceps brachii muscle

(7) triceps brachii muscle
(8) pectoralis major superficialis
(9) pectoralis minor profondus muscle
(10) abdominal external oblique muscle
(11) aponeurosis

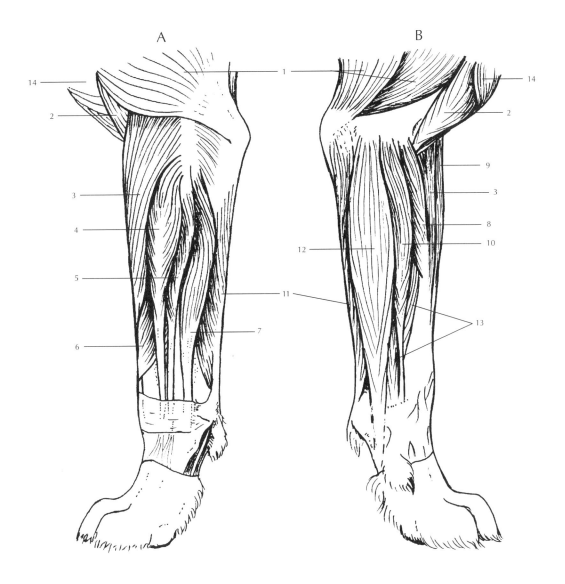

A

B

2.16 Muscles of the Foreleg

(A) Outside
(B) Inside
(1) triceps brachii muscle
(2) biceps brachii muscle
(3) extensor carpi radialis muscle
(4) extensor digitorum communis muscle
(5) extensor digiti minimi muscle
(6) abductor policis longus muscle

(7) extensor carpi ulnaris muscle
(8) pronator teres muscle
(9) brachioradialis muscle
(10) flexor carpi radialis muscle
(11) flexor carpi ulnaris muscle
(12) flexor digitorum sublimis muscle
(13) flexor digitorum profondus muscle
(14) mastoid

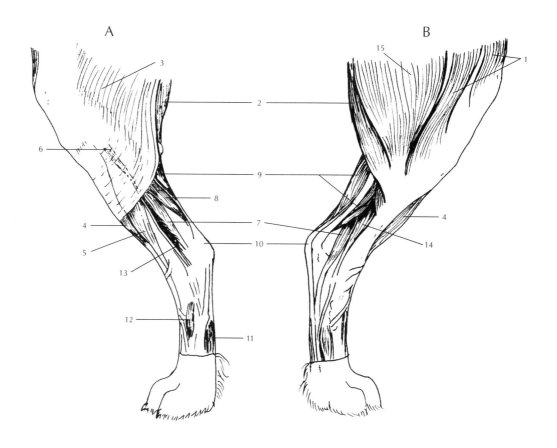

2.17 *Muscles of the Hind Leg*

(A) Outside
(B) Inside
(1) sartorius muscle
(2) semitendinosus muscle
(3) biceps femoris muscle
(4) tibialis anterior muscle
(5) extensor digitorum pedis longus muscle
(6) peroneus longus muscle
(7) flexor hallucis longus muscle

(8) flexor digitorum pedis brevis muscle
(9) gastrocnemius muscle
(10) achilles tendon
(11) interossei muscle
(12) extensor digitorum pedis brevis muscle
(13) peroneus brevis muscle
(14) flexor digitorum pedis longus muscle
(15) gracilis muscle

Trigger points can be found in any muscle of the body. Keep your dog free of trigger points by using the trigger point technique in chapter 8.

Study all the charts in this chapter and learn about all aspects of the dog's body. Understanding the interrelation of the components of the musculoskeletal system will contribute greatly to your expertise in understanding problems and massaging the affected areas.

THE CIRCULATORY SYSTEM

The circulatory system consists of the cardiovascular system and the lymphatic system. The cardiovascular system is made up of the heart, arteries and arterioles, capillaries and veins and venules. The lymphatic system consists of a network of small vessels containing the lymphatic fluid and structures called lymph nodes, which cleanse and filter.

Arterial blood circulation is generated by the pumping action of the heart (80–140 beats per minute in a normal adult dog) and the contraction of the arterial wall muscles sending blood to all body parts. The blood passes into the arterioles (small arteries) and is distributed into the tissues via the capillaries, where the oxygen/carbon dioxide and nutrients/waste exchange occurs. The blood returns via the venules (small veins) and veins. The

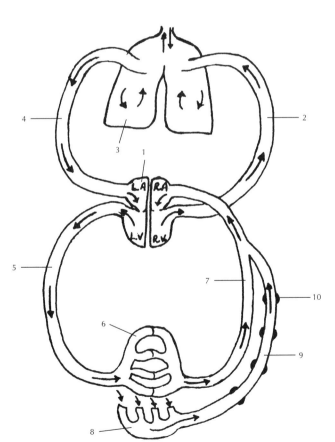

2.18 Circulatory System

(1) heart
(2) pulmonary artery
(3) lungs
(4) pulmonary vein
(5) artery
(6) blood capillaries
(7) vein
(8) lymph capillaries
(9) lymphatic vessel
(10) lymph node

movement of the large locomotor muscle group of the body assists the venous return of blood. Veins are equipped with little cup-like valves to prevent the backward flow of blood. Each muscle contraction squeezes the venous blood in one direction towards the heart. The venous blood passes through the lungs, where it gives up its waste as carbon dioxide gas, and the red blood cells pick up oxygen from the air. Then the blood goes through the heart again and is pumped into the aorta. It takes less than a minute for blood to make its complete round.

Blood contains red blood cells that carry oxygen, white blood cells that fight infection and carry nutrients, and plasma, the yellowish fluid in which both of these types of cell bathe. In addition to those properties blood has several other functions, including the removal of waste products of metabolism, the transport of endocrine secretions, the equalization of water content and temperature regulation.

The lymphatic system is an adjunct to the circulatory system. The lymph vessels pick up the clear, colorless fluid from the interstitial spaces (spaces between cells) that has not been returned through the venous flow. As for the venous return, the return of the lymphatic fluid is assisted by the movement of the large locomotor muscle group of the body. Lymphatics are equipped with little cup-like valves to prevent the backward flow of lymph. Each muscle contraction squeezes the lymphatic fluid in one direction towards the heart where it is dumped into the venous system. A series of filters (lymph nodes) prevent tissue bacteria and foreign matter from re-entering the bloodstream.

The lymphatic system plays an important role in the body's defense mechanism in that it contains lymphocytes, which are the white blood cells that aid in fighting viral and bacterial infections. Edematous swelling occurs as a result of injury, infection or other interference with lymphatic drainage. Lack of exercise can contribute to lymphatic congestion, a condition common in older dogs.

THE RESPIRATORY SYSTEM

The respiratory system includes the nose, mouth, pharynx, windpipe (or trachea), bronchial tubes, bronchioles and lungs.

The lungs, which are somewhat elastic and filled with little sponge-like sacs known as alveoli, are where the blood gives off carbon dioxide and takes on oxygen. The diaphragm is a powerful, large and flat muscle that separates the thoracic and abdominal cavities, and is responsible for the inhalation part of breathing. Exhalation is the relaxing of the diaphragm and the contraction of the rib cage muscles.

THE DIGESTIVE SYSTEM

The digestive system, also known as the alimentary canal, includes the mouth, pharynx, esophagus, stomach, small intestine (duodenum, jejunum and ileum), colon, rectum and anus. The digestive system alters the chemical and physical composition of food so it can be absorbed and utilized by the cells of the body. A healthy digestive tract is vital for efficient assimilation of food.

THE URINARY SYSTEM

The urinary system is made up of the kidneys, ureters, bladder, urethra and penis (male) or vulva (female).

The kidneys, by providing a blood filtering system, remove many waste products and control water balance, pH and the level of many electrolytes. The kidney filtrate, or urine, is conveyed to the bladder by the two ureters and evacuated via the urethra.

THE ENDOCRINE SYSTEM

The endocrine system is made up of glands and associated organs including the hypothalamus, pituitary, thyroid, pancreas, adrenals, liver, kidneys, spleen, ovaries (female) and testes (male).

The endocrine system produces and releases hormones directly into the bloodstream. These hormones regulate growth, development and the function of specific tissues as well as coordinate the metabolic process of the dog.

THE REPRODUCTIVE SYSTEM

The male reproductive system consists of testicles, the accessory glands and ducts, and the external genital organ. The female reproductive system consists of the ovaries, oviducts, uterus, vagina and external genitalia.

The reproductive system ensures the continuation of the species.

3

KINESIOLOGY OF THE DOG

Kinesiology is the study of motion and the structures that make motion possible. This section is for you to use to identify the muscles involved when your animal experiences specific problems.

First, here is a list of some of the terminology that will be used.

* **Protraction:** The forward motion of the legs.

* **Retraction:** The backward motion of the legs.

* **Abduction:** The outward motion of the legs.

* **Adduction:** The inward motion of the legs.

* **Isometric contraction:** This occurs when a muscle contracts without causing an obvious movement. The best example is when a dog stands on a moving platform, like the back of a truck, and has to adjust his muscle distribution to remain standing.

* **Concentric contraction:** This occurs when a muscle shortens as it

contracts and induces articular (joint) movements, such as those seen in protraction, retraction, abduction and adduction movements.

* **Agonist muscle:** A muscle that contracts and is responsible for the concentric contraction.

* **Antagonist muscle:** The muscle that counteracts the agonist action and is elongated during the concentric contraction. The antagonist muscle is often, but not always, responsible for an eccentric contraction.

* **Eccentric contraction:** This takes place when a contracted antagonist muscle releases from its contracted state slowly to allow for better muscle control. Such a contraction permits movement to be slowed down at will. This action avoids jerky movements and allows for elegance and suppleness in the dog's movement. An eccentric contraction also acts as a shock absorber, which is a very important attribute during landing or any other such abrupt movement.

42

HOW A DOG MOVES

To understand how a dog moves, we need to be aware of the interplay between bones, joints, ligaments, tendons and muscle groups that make the movements possible. A dog's hind legs provide the driving force and the power for the movement of the body. The forelegs are more concerned with direction and shock absorption.

Muscles are always arranged in opposing groups performing opposite actions; for example, the extensor muscle group of the foreleg extends the foot during protraction, while the flexor muscle group of the foreleg flexes the same foot during retraction. It is this type of interplay that produces the well-balanced, beautiful motion we love to see in dogs.

PROTRACTION OF THE FORELEG

The muscles involved in the concentric contraction (agonist) that initiates the forward motion of the foreleg are as follows:

1. The brachiocephalic muscle.
2. The pectoralis major superficialis muscle.
3. The mastoid muscle.
4. The biceps brachii muscle.
5. The extensor carpi radialis muscle.
6. The serratus thoracis muscle.

During protraction, the brachiocephalic muscle pulls the shoulder joint up initiating forward movement of the foreleg. At the same time, the serratus thoracis muscle

3.1   Foreleg Protraction

contracts to assist the rotation (back and down) of the top of the scapula. The biceps brachii and mastoid muscles cause flexion of the leg at the elbow. Then the extensor carpi radialis muscle extends the paw as it comes to the ground. The supraspinatus and infraspinatus muscles, the thoracic part of the trapezius muscle, the deltoid muscle and the pectoral muscles all act as stabilizers in the protraction of the foreleg. During the protraction movement, all the muscles involved in the retraction of the foreleg are elongated (antagonist) and throughout their eccentric contraction ensure stability and smoothness of the movement.

RETRACTION OF THE FORELEG

The muscles involved in the concentric contraction (agonist) that initiates the backward motion of the forelegs are as follows:

1. The triceps muscle.

2. The latissimus dorsi muscle.

3. The flexor muscles.

4. The serratus cervicis muscle.

5. The rhomboid muscle.

6. The cervical part of the trapezius muscle.

7. The pectoralis minor profondus muscle.

When the leg is fully protracted, the latissimus dorsi muscle and the triceps muscle are the main muscles responsible for bringing the leg backward. The pectoralis minor profondus muscle pulls backward and toward the center of the dog, contributing to the leg retraction movement and helping

prevent the leg from moving sideways. The play between the cervical and the thoracic part of the serratus muscle allows the scapula to move up and forward. The rhomboid muscle and the cervical part of the trapezius muscle provide extra pull on the top of the scapula. The flexor muscles of the foreleg provide extra push to lift the dog up and forward as the paw leaves the ground for the next stride. As well, the supraspinatus and infraspinatus muscles, and the deltoid muscle act as stabilizers to assist the retraction of the foreleg.

All the muscles (antagonist) involved in the protraction of the foreleg are elongated during the retraction movement and through their eccentric contraction ensure stability and smoothness of action.

ABDUCTION OF THE FORELEG

The muscles responsible for the concentric contraction (agonist) in the abduction of the foreleg are as follows:

1. The supraspinatus and infraspinatus muscles.

2. The deltoid muscle.

3. The rhomboid muscle.

4. The trapezius muscle.

The elongated muscles (antagonist) involved in the abduction of the forelimb are as follows:

1. The pectoralis major superficialis muscle.

2. The pectoralis minor profondus muscle.

3.2   Foreleg Retraction

These muscles attach along the thoracic spine and the scapula and the bones of the foreleg. Their interplay induces the abduction movement. The deltoid, the supraspinatus and infraspinatus muscles pull the point of the shoulder laterally, bringing the leg to the outside. The trapezius and rhomboid muscles assist this movement by pulling on the scapula up toward the top of the shoulder (withers). The pectoral muscle group, in their eccentric contraction, contribute to the stability and smoothness of the movement.

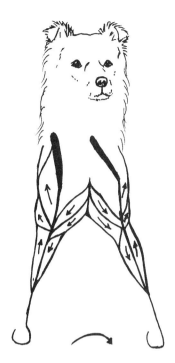

3.3   Foreleg Abduction

3.4   Foreleg Adduction

ADDUCTION OF THE FORELEG

The muscles responsible for the concentric contraction (agonist) in the adduction of the foreleg are as follows:

1. The pectoralis major superficialis muscle.

2. The pectoralis minor profondus muscle.

The elongated muscles (antagonist) involved in the adduction of the foreleg are as follows:

1. The supraspinatus and infraspinatus muscles.

2. The deltoid muscle.

3. The rhomboid muscle.

4. The trapezius muscle.

These agonist muscles attach on the sternum and along the medial aspect of the humerus of the foreleg. The pectoral muscle group is principally responsible for this motion by pulling the leg medially (inward). The antagonist muscles, by their eccentric contraction, contribute to the stability and smoothness of action.

PROTRACTION OF THE HIND LEG

The muscles involved in the concentric contraction (agonist) of the forward motion of the hind leg are as follows:

1. The iliacus muscle (not shown in illustration).

2. The tensor fascial latae muscle.

3. The quadriceps group (lateral vastus) muscle.

4. The sartorius muscle.

5. The biceps femoris muscle.

6. The gastrocnemius muscle.

7. The extensor muscles.

The iliacus muscles run deep from the inside of the pelvis (ilium) and attach to the inside aspect of the femur, below the femoral head. The iliacus muscle initiates the protraction movement by pulling the femur up and forward. This action flexes the hip joint, the stifle joint and the hock joint. The sartorius muscle assists the iliacus by pulling the stifle up and forward. The biceps femoris muscle and the lateral vastus muscle also assist this action by pulling on the stifle joint and tibia, causing the stifle to flex. Also, the contraction of the gastrocnemius muscle allows the flexing of the stifle. The extensor muscles of the hind leg flex the hock joint and extend the paw.

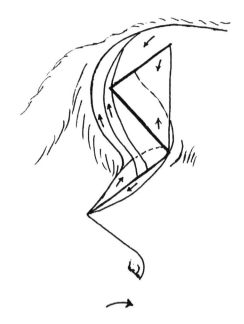

3.5   Hind Leg Protraction

All the muscles involved in the retraction of the hind leg are elongated (antagonist) during the protraction movement, while their eccentric contraction ensure stability and smoothness of action.

RETRACTION OF THE HIND LEG

The muscles involved in the concentric contraction (agonist) of the backward motion of the hind leg are as follows:

1. The gluteus muscles especially the gluteus medius.

2. The hamstring group, which consists of the semi-membranosus, the semi-tendinosus, and biceps femoris muscles.

3. The gastrocnemius muscle.

4. The deep flexors muscle.

The large gluteus medius muscle initiates the retraction movement. The hamstring muscle group is responsible for most of the power of the retraction. The gastrocnemius and the deep flexor muscles assist the flexion of the paw. The quadriceps femoris muscle assists in the extension of the hind leg at the end of the retraction movement. The adductor muscles facilitate this motion by gently pulling the leg medially (inward).

All the muscles involved in the protraction of the hind leg are elongated (antagonist) during the retraction movement, while their eccentric contraction ensure stability and smoothness of action.

ABDUCTION OF THE HIND LEG

The muscles responsible for the concentric contraction (agonist) in the abduction of the hind leg are as follows:

1. The gluteus medius muscle.

2. The gluteus maximus superficialis muscle.

3. The tensor fascia latae muscle.

4. The biceps femoris muscle.

5. The quadriceps femoris muscle.

The elongated muscles (antagonist) involved during the abduction of the hind leg are as follows:

1. The adductor muscle (not shown in illustration).

2. The gracilis muscle.

3.6 Hind Leg Retraction

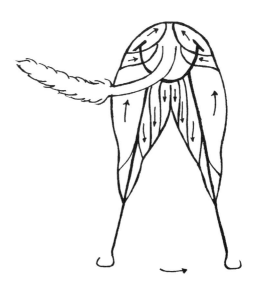

3.7 Hind Leg Abduction

3. The iliacus muscle (not shown in illustration).

These muscles attach along the bones of the hind leg and their interplay causes the abduction movement. The tensor fascia latae muscle pulls the stifle laterally (outward). The movement is maintained by the action of the gluteus muscles, the biceps femoris and the quadriceps femoris muscle all pulling on the femur bone laterally (outward). The antagonist muscles, by their eccentric contraction, contribute to the smoothness of action.

ADDUCTION OF THE HIND LEG

The muscles responsible for the concentric contraction (agonist) in the adduction of the hind leg are as follows:

1. The adductor muscles (not shown in illustration).

2. The gracilis muscle.

3. The iliacus muscle (not shown in illustration).

The antagonist muscles involved in the adduction of the hind leg are as follows:

1. The gluteus muscles.

2. The biceps femoris muscle.

3. The quadriceps femoris muscle.

4. The tensor fascia latae muscle.

These muscles attach along the bones of the hind leg. Their interplay causes the adduction movement. The adductor muscles and the gracilis muscle are

3.8   Hind Leg Adduction

mainly responsible for this action by pulling the hind leg medially (inward). The iliacus muscle assists this action. The antagonist muscles, by their eccentric contraction, contribute to the smoothness of the movement.

THE VERTEBRAL COLUMN

In addition to protecting the spinal cord, the vertebral column provides a frame-like structure made up of strong bones and very thick ligaments. The vertical column's role is to bridge the anterior and posterior limbs, to offer solid anchoring for the strong muscle groups, and to protect the spinal nerve root.

EXTENSION OF THE VERTEBRAL COLUMN

The agonist muscles responsible for the extension of the column are located above the spinal column. This extensor muscle group is made up of:

1. The spinalis dorsi muscle.
2. The longissimus dorsi muscle.
3. The iliocostalis dorsi muscle.

FLEXION OF THE VERTEBRAL COLUMN

All the muscles below the spinal column are known as the column's flexors. The abdominal muscles (see Figure 2.14) play an important role as flexors of the spine, but so do the muscle groups involved in attaching the limbs to the spine. To some degree, the intercostal muscles assist in the flexion of the spine as well. The muscles associated with protraction, retraction, abduction and adduction of the limbs also have a second function of supporting the backbone.

LATERAL FLEXION OF THE VERTEBRAL COLUMN

Lateral flexion, or side-to-side bending, is not caused by any specific muscle. In fact, such bending is the result of a unilateral (one sided) concentric contraction of either the flexor or extensor muscles of the spine previously mentioned. In this movement, the intervertebral muscles (not shown in illustration) play a signifi-cant role. Running from one vertebrae to the next, the intervertebral muscles are tiny muscles along each side of the verte-bral column. The grand oblique muscle of

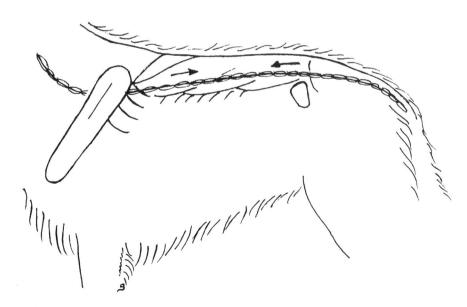

3.9 Back Extension

the abdominal group, especially the internal oblique, also is an important player in this lateral flexion movement.

THE RIB CAGE

The pectoral muscles and the serratus muscles play an essential role in supporting and stabilizing the rib cage, or chest, in relation to the spine. The abdominal muscles assist lateral bending as well as support of the rib cage. The intercostal muscles are responsible for the actual movement of the ribs. The diaphragm muscle is responsible for breathing.

THE NECK MUSCLES

The neck muscles play a vital role in locomotion. Most obvious when running, but also seen in trotting or walking, the downward swing of the head helps to lift the rear legs off the ground as the dog moves forward. The neck muscles are as follows:

1. The splenius muscle.

2. The occipitalis muscle.

3. The rhomboid muscle.

4. The serratus cervicis muscle.

5. The trapezius muscle (cervical part).

6. The rectus capitis ventralis muscle.

7. The sternohyoidei muscle.

8. The brachiocephalicus muscle.

9. The mastoid muscle.

10. The sternomastoid muscle.

11. The levator scapulae muscle.

12. The intervertebral muscles (not shown in illustration).

These muscles are attached along the spine from the base of the skull, down the cervical vertebrae to the thoracic vertebrae, to the upper ribs and the scapulas. Their interplay will induce several different movements.

EXTENSION OF THE NECK

The neck muscles involved in the concentric contraction (agonist) of the extension of the neck are as follows:

1. The splenius muscle.

2. The occipitalis muscle.

3.10   Neck Extension

3. The rhomboid muscle.

4. The trapezius muscle (cervical part).

5. The serratus cervicis muscle.

6. The rectus capitis ventralis muscle.

As these muscles contract, they cause the cervical section of the spine to arch in extension bringing the head upward. All the muscles involved in the flexion of the neck are elongated (antagonist) during the extension movement, while their eccentric contraction ensure the stability and smoothness of the movement.

FLEXION OF THE NECK

The neck muscles involved in the concentric contraction (agonist) of the flexion of the neck are as follows:

1. The sternohyoidei muscle.

2. The brachiocephalicus muscle.

3. The mastoid muscle.

4. The sternomastoid muscle.

5. The levator scapulae muscle.

As these muscles contract, they cause the cervical section of the spine to bend forward in flexion bringing the head downward. All the muscles involved in the extension of the neck are elongated (antagonist) during the flexion movement, while their eccentric contraction ensure stability and smoothness of action.

LATERAL FLEXION OF THE NECK

The lateral flexion of the neck is the result of an unilateral (one side only) concentric contraction of either flexor or extensor muscles of the neck. Such unilateral contraction will cause the head and the spinal column to rotate to the same side. The play between the flexors and extensors will allow the dog to rotate upward or downward. The intervertebral

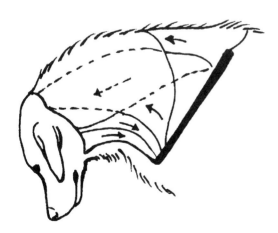

3.11   Neck Flexion

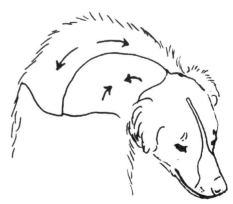

3.12   Lateral Neck Flexion

muscles play a significant role in the torque of the neck. All the muscles involved on the opposite side of the neck are elongated (antagonist), while their eccentric contraction ensure the stability and smoothness of the movement.

Knowing which muscles are involved in which movement will give you great confidence in your assessment and treatment of the animal. This knowledge will greatly contribute to the success of your work.

4

In this chapter we will explain the benefits of stretching and demonstrate the stretching exercises that you can add to your massage routine. Dogs stretch spontaneously and naturally, tuning up their muscles and keeping their joints flexible. In normal conditions, a dog will not overstretch. Regular stretching can prevent muscle problems, provide relaxation and develop your dog's body awareness. Stretching will improve your dog's coordination as well as give you feedback on his physical condition. It is important to note that if your dog has had any recent physical problems (a fall or direct trauma) or surgery, particularly of the joints and muscles, consult your veterinarian before you start a stretching program.

The benefits of regular stretching exercises are both physical and cerebral (mental).

PHYSICAL BENEFITS

The apparent musculoskeletal benefit of frequent stretching exercises result in increased flexibility, in prevention of injuries, in improved general metabolism and in better movements.

❖ **Flexibility:** Stretching keeps the muscle fibers and the joints flexible. When you stretch a muscle, you lengthen its fibers. This action mechanically affects the Golgi sensory nerve cells and the muscle spindle sensory nerve cells, resetting the feedback mechanism to the central nervous system (see chapter 2). The results are vasodilation and tonification of the fibers. Stretching also improves the tone of the muscle fibers and the elasticity of the ligaments and the joint capsules. Stretching reduces muscle tension and therefore prevents muscle pulls. A strong, pre-stretched muscle resists stress better than a strong, unstretched muscle. Better elasticity of the muscles, tendons and ligaments allows for freer, easier, more controlled and quicker movements—all resulting in better overall coordination.

❖ **Prevention of injuries:** Stretching not only prevents muscle strain, ligament sprain and loosens the joint capsules, but it also makes the body feel more relaxed. Stretching releases muscle contracture due to old scar tissue, helps relieve muscle pain from chronic tension and reduces post–exercise soreness and stiffness.

❖ **Metabolism:** Muscle stretching increases blood and lymph circulation and brings more oxygen and nutrients to the body parts. It also prevents inflammation and adhesion (scar tissue) formation, trigger point formation and stress point buildup.

❖ **Gait Improvement:** Regular stretching will improve the range of motion of the joints, the stride length, the overall coordination and the response time of the reflexes. The physiological benefits of stretching exercises upon the body are immediate. You should regularly add them to your massage work.

Cerebral Benefits

Cerebral refers to the nervous system control—the brain, the spinal cord and the nerve plexus. A dog's "body awareness" is, of course, cerebral (mental). Hence, one part of stretching is cerebral because the activity develops body awareness. As you stretch various body parts, you help your dog to focus on them and to become mentally in touch with them. This process develops the animal's self-awareness thereby improving coordination in all aspects of movement.

The stretching of muscles sends relaxation impulses—via sensory nerves—to the central nervous system, reflexively loosening the dog's mind control over his body. Stretching will also decrease motor nerve tension transmitted throughout the body. The animal will relax both physically and mentally. This is an important message factor when dealing with animals who have been in accidents, have been frightened or are in pain. Stretching will indirectly help dogs to release the anxiety associated with muscle tension.

Stretching will give you feedback on the state of health of the muscle groups and of the ligament structures, particularly in regard to their elasticity and tone.

When to Stretch

Warning! Always stretch when the dog is warm.

Muscles, tendons and ligaments (and eventually joint capsules) risk damage if stretched when cold. Stretching a dog after a warm-up (walk/trot) period will limit the risk of injury from overstretching. It is best to stretch as cooldowns immediately after playing or training. Again, if your animal has had any recent physical problems or surgery (particularly of the joints and muscles) or if he has been inactive or sedentary for some time, consult your veterinarian before you start a stretching program.

Observing the preceding warning, you can stretch your dog at any time. Stretching should be done every day, after every play or training session, and should be included with your massage work. A regular routine will give you feedback on the physical condition of your dog, the flexibility of his joints, the agility of his muscle groups, the progression of the animal's training program and the effects of your massage treatments.

If you need to stretch a specific area during a localized massage treatment for a handicapped dog, that area can be warmed up with a hot towel, a hot water bottle (see chapter 5) or simply by massage (see the SEW approach in chapter 8).

THE STRETCH REFLEX

The stretch reflex is a protective mechanism that prevents a muscle from being overstretched and torn. The stretch reflex is a nervous reaction caused when the muscle spindle, a sensory nerve cell, is overstretched (see chapter 2). When overstretched, the muscle spindle fires nerve impulses to the spinal cord. The reflex arc mechanism (located in the spine) then fires back motor nerve impulses that cause an instant muscle contraction. This contraction prevents the muscle from being injured. So, do not overstretch, do not try to reach beyond the muscle's maximum flexibility. Instead, just hold the stretch in a relaxed manner and for a longer period of time. The dog's flexibility will increase naturally when you start stretching regularly.

HOW TO STRETCH

To attain best results, you need to respect the structures you are working on. To manipulate correctly, it is important to be concerned with the animal's natural body alignment. Always move and stretch the dog's limb according to its natural range of motion. Do not exert torque or abnormal twist.

Stretching is not a contest to see how far you can stretch or how much more to do each time you do it. The object of stretching is to relax muscle and ligament tension in order to promote freer movement and to trigger the other benefits listed earlier. To achieve all of this, you need to stretch safely, starting with the easy stretch described in this chapter and building to a regular, deeper stretch. Never go too far, the stretch reflex will cause the muscle to contract to prevent tearing of the fibers.

Stretching should always be done in a relaxed and steady manner. The first time you stretch your dog, do it slowly and gently. Give the dog time to adjust his body and mind to the physical and the nervous stress release that stretching initiates. The stretch should be tailored to the animal's particular muscular structure, flexibility and varying tension levels. Again, because you will risk tearing the muscle and ligament fibers, do not overstretch.

When you release a stretch, gently return the leg in its original position. Note that many dogs show varying degrees of sensitivity to handling. Understand that how you handle your dog from the beginning has a definite impact on how you will be able to handle him in the future. Make a distinction between a reaction to pain and an objection to handling.

THE EASY STRETCH

Always start with the easy stretch, which means stretching only 75 to 80 percent of the total stretching capability of that particular body part and holding the stretch for 10 to 20 seconds. Your dog will enjoy this gentle approach. Be steady in the development of your work. Never work hastily or with jerky movements. Do not pull excessively on the leg because you risk tearing muscle fibers by overstretching.

For example, take hold of your dog's foreleg gently and guide it through its forward range of motion, bringing it to its natural point of stretch. There you should feel a mild tension and at that point release your traction slightly. That is the easy stretch. Be relaxed as you hold the stretch. Hold the position for 10 seconds during which the tension should subside. Then gently return the leg to its natural position.

THE DEEPER STRETCH

Once the dog gets used to the easy stretch, you can work into the deeper stretch. Start with the easy stretch. Past the initial 10 seconds and as the muscle tightness decreases adjust your traction until you again feel a mild tension. Hold for another 5 seconds. If your dog does not mind, repeat two to three times until you feel you have reached the maximum stretching capacity of the muscle. Do not exceed one minute on any given stretch. Avoid triggering the stretch reflex by overstretching. Be in control.

SPONTANEOUS STRETCH

Often during the development stretch and sometimes during the easy stretch, the dog will spontaneously stretch himself fully for a few seconds (3 to 5 seconds). This is a definite sign that the animal is enjoying the stretch and that the dog needs it very much. As you hold the limb during such spontaneous release, you can feel all the deep tension coming out as a vibration; it is quite an experience. After such a release, there is no need to hold the stretch further. Bring the limb back to its natural position.

MENTAL COUNTING

The time frame in which you stretch a muscle is very important. At first, silently count the seconds for each stretch. This will ensure that you hold tension for the correct length of time. After a while, you will develop a feel for this practice and will subconsciously know when the animal has reached its full stretching capability without having to count. This practice of mental counting will help you get the best results from the stretching technique. Be aware of the dog's reaction to the stretch before you repeat the exercise. You should also investigate if any undue stress points or trigger points are present; release them with the proper massage technique (see chapter 8).

GENERAL STRETCHING OUTLINE

First start with the easy stretch for 10 to 15 seconds, and then work into the deeper stretch. This activity will finely tune the muscles and increase overall flexibility. Do not overstretch, do not make jerky or bouncy movements. Never stretch an acutely (recently) torn muscle. Never force the joint in any abnormal range or twist it. Always stretch the agonist muscle (the one responsible for the action) and its antagonist muscle (the one that has to let go for the action to happen). A regular practice of stretching with comfortable and painless movements will help you go beyond your dog's current flexibility limit and come closer to his full potential.

THE STRETCHING ROUTINE

FORELEG STRETCHES

There are three foreleg stretches: the forward stretch, the backward stretch, and shoulder rotation.

FORWARD STRETCH

This protraction movement will stretch the muscle involved in the retraction of

4.1   Foreleg Forward Stretch: *This protraction stretching movement is good for stretching the flexor muscles of the leg.*

4.2   Foreleg Forward Stretch

the foreleg. Pick up the leg above the paw with one hand and place the other behind the elbow. Gently bring the leg forward and upward. This stretch will affect the muscles of the shoulder, the trapezius, the rhomboid, the latissimus dorsi, the serratus cervicis, the deltoid and the triceps. Once the dog is well into the stretch, maintain the tension with one hand behind and above the wrist, and with

your other hand extend the paw. This action will deepen the stretch of the flexor tendons. Be gentle and cautious.

BACKWARD STRETCH

The retraction movement will stretch the muscles involved in the protraction of the foreleg. With one hand pick up the leg

4.3 Foreleg Backward Stretch: *This retraction stretching movement is good for stretching the foreleg extensor muscles.*

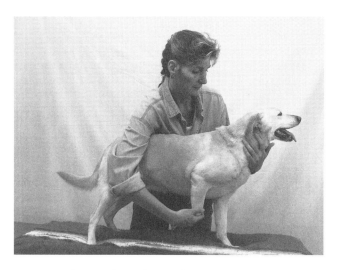

4.4 Foreleg Backward Stretch

above the paw. Place the other hand in front and below the elbow joint. Gently bring the leg backward until the radius bone is at a 90° angle with the ground. This is a good stretch for the muscle of the chest and the upper leg, specifically, the pectorals, the brachiocephalicus, the biceps and the extensors.

Once the dog is well into the stretch, maintain the tension with one hand in front and above the wrist, and with your other hand flex the paw. This action will deepen the stretch of the extensor tendons. Be gentle and cautious.

SHOULDER ROTATION

The following variation will help loosen deep muscles such as the pectorals, the serratus cervices and thoracis, the intercostal fascia and to relax the ligaments of the shoulder girdle structure. Slide one hand between the chest and the forearm, and with your other hand grab gently the lower foreleg above the paw. Start a circular movement moving the leg inward, then forward, outward and back. Repeat three to five times and then reverse the movement. Avoid excessive pressure at the shoulder joint.

THE HIND LEG STRETCHES

There are three hind leg stretches: the forward stretch, the backward stretch, and the hind leg transverse stretch.

FORWARD STRETCH

This protraction movement (also known as the hamstring stretch) will stretch the

muscles involved in the retraction of the hind leg. With one hand pick up the paw. Position your other hand below and behind the hock joint, and gently move the leg forward in its natural line of movement. While the leg is forward you may consider moving it a little inward. Do not move the hind leg to the outside because this is not a natural movement; it could adversely affect the hip joint. This is a good stretch for the muscles of the hip and thighs, the tensor fascia latae, the gluteus and the hamstring muscles (the semi-tendinosus, the semi-membranosus and the biceps femoris). Once comfortable in the stretch, you can consider extending the paw to deepen the stretch over the flexor tendons. Be gentle and cautious.

BACKWARD STRETCH

This retraction movement will stretch the muscles involved in the flexion of the hip and of the leg. With one hand pick up the paw and place your other hand in front of the hock joint. Bring the leg back through its natural range until you feel the stretch. Once comfortable in the stretch, you can consider flexing the paw to deepen the stretch over the extensor tendons. Be gentle and cautious. This is a good stretch for the following muscles: the iliacus, the sartorius, the tensor fascia latae, the quadriceps femoris, the extensor and the abdominal muscles.

HIND LEG TRANSVERSE STRETCH

This is another movement to stretch the quadriceps femoris muscle of the hind leg and the TFL (tensor fascia latae muscle).

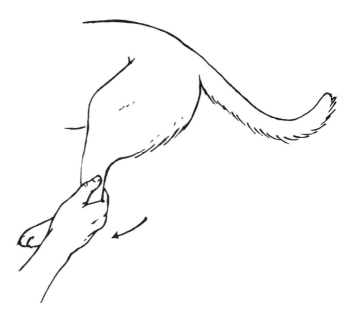

4.5 Hind Leg Forward Stretch: *This protraction stretching movement is good for stretching the flexor muscles of the hind leg.*

4.6 Hind Leg Forward Stretch

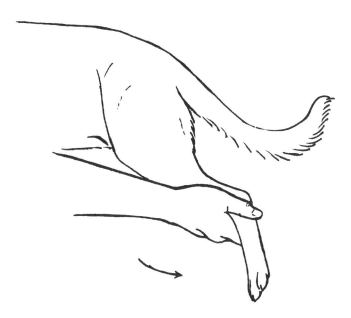

4.7 *Hind Leg Backwards Stretch:* *This retraction stretching movement is good for stretching the extensor muscles of the hind leg.

4.8 *Hind Leg Backwards Stretch*

Grasp the rear leg above the paw on the opposite side of the dog and bring the leg under the belly and slightly toward opposite front paw. Be aware of the torque you will produce on the hock and the stifle joint by stretching this way. Do not apply too much pressure. Be gentle, paying attention to your dog's comfort.

4.9   *Hind Leg Transverse Stretch:* *This special stretching movement is good for stretching the quadriceps and gluteus muscle groups and the tensor fascia latae muscle.*

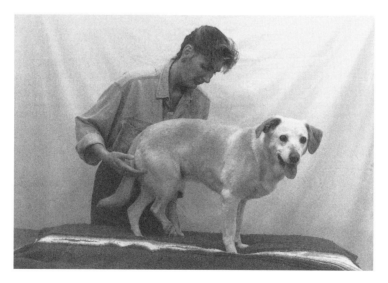

4.10   *Hind Leg Transverse Stretch*

THE BACK MUSCLES

There is no particular stretching movement for the back muscles, but, by reflex, you can affect these muscles by pressing your thumb into the belly region, right over the attachment tendon of the pectoralis minor profondus muscle on the sternum bone. This will cause the dog to tuck up, thereby rounding its back and stretching the following muscles: longissimus dorsi, iliocostalis and the spinalis dorsi. Also tickling the belly will cause the same reflex. This is one of the easiest stretches.

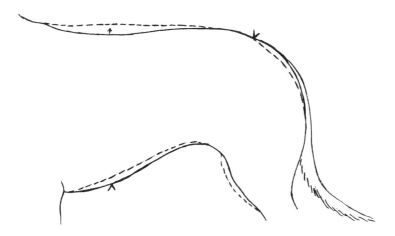

4.11   Back Muscles Stretch

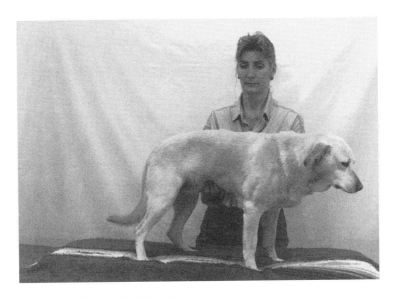

4.12   Back Muscles Stretch

Another way to affect these muscles is to stimulate the sacrum area along its edges with some thumb point pressure moves. This will cause a reflex action in the abdominal muscles that will result in an arching of the back structure and a stretching of the back muscles.

TAIL STRETCH

Stretching the tail is a great way to produce a feeling of deep relaxation in your dog. This stretch is a major part of the relaxation massage routine (see chapter 9). When approaching the rear, use gentle strokes along the tail bone and down the buttocks before picking up the tail with one of your hands. Leave your other hand on the sacrum. Take hold of the tail a few inches from its base and gently move it in a circle starting clockwise, two or three times. Repeat in the counterclockwise direction two or three times. During these movements, take note of any restriction found in moving the tail to either side.

At this point, move to the back of the dog and very gently pull on the tail (use common sense, don't pull to the point of discomfort). Hold this stretch for approximately one minute unless the dog shows discomfort. Usually the dog, feeling good, responds positively by pulling against your traction or lowering his head.

Using light muscle-squeezing moves between the thumb and fingers of your right hand, gently squeeze each vertebrae from the base of the tail down. Keep stretching with the left hand. Reverse hands if that is more suitable to you. Make

note of the tail's flexibility looking for sore spots and possible inflammation. Release the stretch progressively and then stroke the hindquarters and sacrum area for a few seconds.

Warning! At the start of your stretching routine, if the tail feels loose with a "give" of one-quarter to one-half an inch, stop immediately—the dog has a joint problem at the tail junction. This condition in a dog is not uncommon; stretching would trigger pain and could result in a strain of the tail attachment site.

If the dog shows discomfort, inflammation or abnormal symptoms with palpation of this area prior to your stretching, the stretching would be contraindicated. Check with your veterinarian.

NECK STRETCHES

These neck stretches will affect all aspects of the neck's muscles. You can do all stretches using an incentive such as a piece of a dog biscuit. This makes the work much, much easier.

LATERAL STRETCH

Allow the dog to sniff the "incentive" and guide it toward the side/back. This movement will stretch the neck's extensor and flexor muscles on the opposite side. You can increase the lateral stretch by asking your dog to stretch further toward the point of the hip. Talk softly to your dog as you guide him into the stretch. Do both the right and left sides.

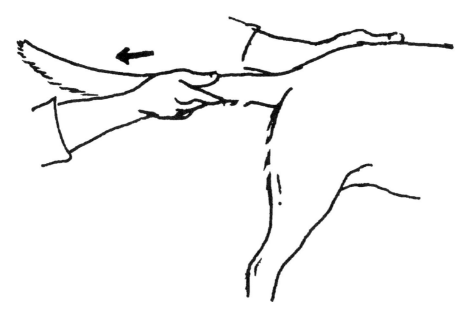

4.13   Tail Stretch

4.14   Tail Stretch

4.15   Lateral Neck Stretch: *Duplicate on other side; use food rewards to make the work much easier.*

4.16   Lateral Neck Stretch

NECK FLEXION STRETCH

As with the lateral stretch, use an incentive to guide your dog's head down in between his legs. In performing this particular stretch, you can add a variation: as you bring the head down move it either to the right or to the left. Thus the extensor muscles will be thoroughly stretched.

4.17   Neck Flexion: *Use a food reward.*

4.18   Neck Flexion

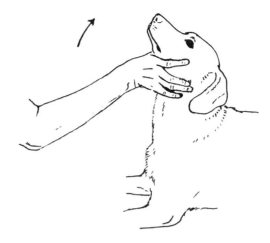

4.19 Neck Extension: *Progressively bring the head into this position.*

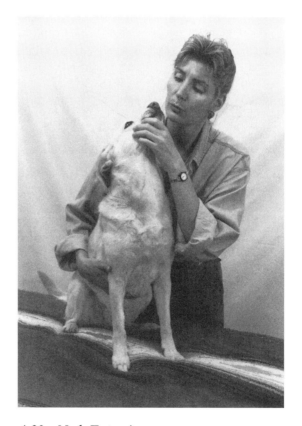

4.20   Neck Extension

NECK EXTENSION STRETCH

As with the other neck stretches, use an incentive to guide your dog's head upward and out as far as it can go. This movement will stretch the neck's flexor muscles.

Regular stretching exercises will contribute greatly to the dog's overall flexibility and fitness. They should be part of the dog's regular exercise program. Done individually, stretching will assist you in the application and success of your massage treatments.

5

HYDROTHERAPY

This chapter explains the benefits and demonstrates the application of hydrotherapy, which means water treatment applied externally to the body. Using hydrotherapy before and after massage treatments will increase the effectiveness of your work.

Heat and cold are used to relieve pain in acute or chronic conditions and in inflammatory disorders for both humans and animals. Heat and cold are still the best treatment in the practice of pain control. No other methods are as effective, as safe and easy to use, as free from side effects and as cost effective. Because they affect the cutaneous nerve endings, both heat and cold decrease pain and muscle tension. Accomplished through opposite physical effects, they are used at different stages of an injury's development (for example, cold in acute stage, heat in chronic condition).

Hydrotherapy comes in a number of forms depending upon the temperature of the water, the method of application, the duration of treatment and so on. When you apply hydrotherapy to your

dog, always monitor the entire process, checking feedback signs at all times, being ready to adjust your treatment if any discomfort arises.

Water applications produce two effects: a first, temporary effect and a second, more lasting effect. For example, cold first constricts the blood vessels and numbs the nerve endings (pain control). Then, it triggers a lasting dilation of the vessels. Heat first dilates the blood vessels and soothes the nerve endings; then, it causes a lasting relaxation of the tissues.

Water application temperatures are classified in the table on the opposite page.

DURATION OF TREATMENT

The more extreme the temperature, the shorter the application's duration; the more moderate the temperature, the more prolonged the application. A very short duration is about 5 to 15 seconds, a short duration is between 15 and 60 seconds, an average duration is about 2 minutes, a prolonged duration is between 3 and 10 minutes, a very prolonged duration is from 10 to 30 minutes.

STAGES OF RECOVERY

In therapy, there are three approximate stages in the recovery process of an injury: the acute stage, the subacute stage and the chronic stage. These definitions are not totally exact as there are also in-between stages.

THE ACUTE STAGE

The first 24 hours following an injury is the acute stage. Use cold immediately. This will stop hemorrhaging in the damaged tissues and will contribute to reducing the swelling before you commence your message. You can apply cold as ice (in a solid form or crushed with some water in a plastic bag) or as cold running water.

THE SUBACUTE STAGE

The time between 24 and 72 hours is considered the subacute stage. By then, the injury has usually stabilized. Use the vascular flush—the alternation of cold and heat applications—several minutes for each application. Immediately after a massage, you may apply some cold to soothe tender tissues.

THE IN-BETWEEN STAGES

Closer to the acute stage, in the first 24 to 48 hours, first apply cold for 3 minutes, then apply heat for 2 minutes. Repeat this

WATER TEMPERATURE	
Cold	40 to 60°F (4.4 to 15.5°C)
Cool	65 to 75°F (18.3 to 23.8°C)
Tepid	85 to 95°F (29.4 to 35°C)
Warm	90 to 100°F (32.2 to 37.7°C)
Hot	100 to 110°F (37.7 to 43.3°C)

WARNING: For hot applications, the temperature should be 5 to 12°C (41 to 53.6°F) above normal body temperature. Water temperatures between 43 and 50°C (109.4 to 122°F) should be safe. *Above 50°C, 122°F, you risk burning the skin.* Use a thermometer to be sure.

cycle 2 or 3 times. Always finish with cold. Follow with a light effleurage toward the heart or simply use stroking if the body part appears to be too sensitive.

When closer to the chronic stage (48 to 72 hours), first apply heat for 3 minutes, then apply cold for 2 minutes. Repeat 2 or 3 times. Always finish with cold for 2 minutes. Follow with a light effleurage toward the heart or use light stroking if the body part appears to be too sensitive.

THE CHRONIC STAGE

Beyond 72 hours, in the chronic stage, use heat to loosen the tissues and to increase blood circulation. After a massage, you may apply some cold to soothe the tender tissues, especially if you have worked them deeply.

When an old chronic injury flares up, soreness with some degree of inflammation and eventually some swelling may occur at the site. In this case, use cold hydrotherapy to relieve the edema and numb the irritated nerve endings. This action will reduce the inflammation and allow you to work more easily. You may use a vascular flush as well, always finishing with cold.

Consider the situation well. If you choose to use cold water over a large area (for example, to deal with inflammation of the back), do not apply it if the dog is cold or chilled. Help your dog warm up first with a short walk or play. However, if a cold water treatment is to be used over a local area (for example, in the case of tendonitis), the warming up of that area can simply be achieved by massage (wringings and effleurages).

COLD

Cold is widely used in emergencies right after an injury or a trauma to stop any bleeding, prevent excessive swelling and lower the pain level. Cold can also be applied during the flare-up of old chronic injuries to reduce inflammation and pain symptoms.

EFFECTS OF COLD

Cold water application first chills the skin. This causes the constriction of the blood capillaries, the lymph channels, the muscular and the elastic tissues contained in the dermis. This constriction drives the blood to the interior, reducing circulation and preventing swelling in the trauma area. Cold also decreases pain by numbing the sensory nerve endings.

After the cold is removed, there comes a secondary reaction. The blood capillaries expand, allowing blood to return to the body's surface. This reaction is the body's defense mechanism responding to warm the entire body. If the treatment is applied to the entire body, circulation will be stimulated over the entire system. This stimulation will raise the body's temperature, raise the blood pressure, contract the muscles, strengthen the heart action, stimulate the nervous system, stimulate the metabolism, and slow and deepen breathing.

Prolonged cool applications produce similar effects to cold, but these are not as marked and the reaction is thus not quite as pronounced.

APPLICATION OF COLD

Ice packs and other cold applications may be used for contusions and sprains during the first 24 hours. Cold reduces hemorrhaging and swelling in the damaged fibers. It also contributes to controlling pain by activating endorphin production.

In treating acute problems be careful not to lower the temperature too much by excessive cold or prolonged water treatments. A "cold reaction" may follow. Cover the dog with a blanket.

Cold is also used in chronic cases to decrease pain in very tender areas or to reduce the swelling in a chronically inflamed area (for example, tendonitis, bursitis, arthritis). By absorbing heat from the irritated area, cold reduces the metabolic rate thereby keeping the inflammation low, reducing the incidence of muscle spasm and reducing nerve irritation by slowing down the velocity of nerve conduction. All of this breaks the pain–spasm–pain cycle. Cold is used extensively in the control of inflamed tendons and joint structures.

Cold water should be used to relieve burn pain. Immediately immerse the burned area in very cold or ice water, or spray cold water over the area until the animal is pain free. Check with your veterinarian.

COLD DEVICES AND TECHNIQUES

Several cooling devices are used in cold therapy:

❖ Specially designed, Velcro-equipped leg wraps containing chemical ice bags. These leg wraps are easy to assemble and are very convenient when traveling.

❖ Specially designed leg boots that can be filled with cold water.

❖ The most widely known and very practical application is cold water hosing (spraying or bathing).

❖ Containers of cold water are very practical and popular. To remove toxins from the skin and keep swelling down some people add apple cider vinegar and sea salt to the water.

❖ Crushed ice and water in a plastic bag wrapped in a towel, applied to the skin and held with a bandage is very practical and inexpensive.

❖ Cold poultices are very effective in relieving tendon inflammation. They are made with a semi-solid mixture of clay in a cotton cloth and applied cold to the body part.

❖ A cotton towel wrung out in cold water and kept in a refrigerator or freezer can be wrapped around a leg or joint to reduce inflammation. Hold in place with a leg wrap or pin.

❖ A cold towel or a cold mitten applied with large friction movements over the whole body will produce a stimulating, tonic effect.

❖ Sponging with cool water is a quick way to cool off a dog during exercise.

THE ICE CUP MASSAGE

Take a 4- to 8-ounce paper or Styrofoam cup, fill it with water and freeze it. Hold the cup by the bottom, peel the rim away and apply the ice on the coat to massage the area in a circular motion. The rhythm should not be too slow nor too fast, approximately 4 seconds for every 5-inch circle. The pressure should be light (1 or 2 pounds). The application should last for 1 or 2 minutes for a small dog and up to 5 minutes maximum for a large dog. Observe the structure, the degree of swelling, the inflammation present in the tissues and the tenderness of the tissues. Be careful not to cause ice burns. Follow with a light massage (strokings, effleurages, gentle kneadings) or wrap the area with some cloth to regenerate warmth quickly. This technique is very useful when dealing with any swelling and inflammation in the leg. It is easily available, easily transported, easily applicable and is inexpensive.

DURATION OF COLD APPLICATION

Cold should be applied for a prolonged duration lasting approximately 10 minutes, but no longer than 15 minutes. Direct ice application such as ice massage should be of average duration. It should not last more than 2 or 3 minutes when applied directly over a thin coat, or up to 5 minutes when over a thick coat. Use an average duration, 2 or 3 minutes application, for very sensitive body parts such as the face or groin.

Cold hydrotherapy applications are easily available, easy to work with, inexpensive and very effective. Have some ice cups and wet towels ready for use in your freezer. It pays to be ready for emergencies! Include this procedure in your preventive therapy, before and after your massages; it will make your work easier and more effective.

HEAT

Heat is invaluable in therapy. Heat is used by veterinarians and other trained professionals at every level in the medical practice—not only in hydrotherapy, but also with ultrasound, lasers, heating lamps and so on. In combination with massage therapy, heat greatly helps in the recovery stages of injuries, as well as in maintenance and preventive programs.

EFFECTS OF HEAT

Heat first decreases pain by soothing the sensory nerve endings. Heat causes vasodilation of blood and lymph channels resulting in improved circulation, bringing more oxygen and nutrients to the structures, as well as assisting in the removal of toxins. Heat loosens fibers (muscle, tendon, ligament), dislodges toxins and prepares the subject area for a good massage. Moist heat is more effective than dry heat because it penetrates more deeply into the body.

Another effect of heat is to bring a general feeling of relaxation to the muscle fibers, tendons and ligaments. Heat raises the body temperature, increases skin activity, stimulates the metabolism and lowers the blood pressure.

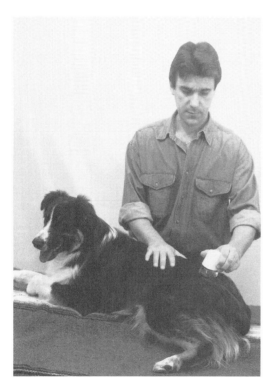

5.1 Ice Massage Technique: *After peeling the rim of the foam or paper cup, proceed to the ice massage application, here on the hip.*

APPLICATION OF HEAT

Heat is used mostly in subacute or chronic cases of post traumatic recovery. Heat is used to soften the aches of old wounds, to ease low-grade inflammations, and to relieve stiffness in older animals. Used widely in deep massage treatments, heat loosens muscle fibers and other fibrous tissues prior to friction moves.

Heat may be used to control pain in acute injuries. If heat is used on contusions, sprains and other acute injuries, it should be as hot as can be tolerated, usually above 48°C (118°F). At a high temperature such as this, heat works as effectively as ice packs because of its great ability to stop bleeding into the tissues.

HEAT DEVICES AND TECHNIQUES

Here are some heat devices and techniques that you can use:

❖ A hot water bottle is very effective.

❖ Heat lamps are efficient but require special installations.

❖ Electrical heating pads are not recommended. They may cause burns and are potentially dangerous because they are a chewing hazard.

❖ Hydrocollator packs are probably the most convenient. These packs contain mud and are preheated in hot water containers. Wrap them in a towel before you apply them to your dog. Be careful that the temperature is not so high that it burns the animal's skin (no more than 12°C/53.6°F above normal body temperature).

❖ Hot towels are very convenient but need to be replaced regularly. Penetrating deeper into the muscle layers, wet or moist heat is generally more effective than dry heat. When applying hot towels, cover them with plastic to ensure an accumulation of body heat.

❖ Poultices are very effective. Poultices produce moist heat from a semi-solid mixture of various substances such as clay, flax seed or mustard applied to the body while hot.

❖ Counter-irritant liniments produce heat effectively, but they should be used very cautiously. Ask your veterinarian first, because there is a risk of skin irritation. Also, such liniment applications should be covered to prevent the dog from licking the product off or rubbing it into its eyes.

DURATION OF HEAT APPLICATION

Prolonged to very prolonged applications (10 to 20 minutes) are the rule for temperatures under 48°C (110°F). Because of the risk of overheating, no more than 20 minutes should be applied at a time. Very hot heat (over 48°C/110°F) should be applied very carefully and for only a very short duration of from 5 to 15 seconds. When hot heat is used to stop hemorrhaging, a short to average duration of 1 or 2 minutes is appropriate.

5.2   Heat Application: *A hot water bottle, wrapped in towel, applied over the hips.*

Too much heat applied too long can irritate nerve endings and result in neuralgia, which is a dull to severe ache in the nerve endings. If you suspect such a case has arisen, use cool cloths to numb those nerve endings and to bring back normal sensations. Also remember that a dog with a thick coat of hair may be less sensitive to heat applied externally.

Warning: Never apply heat to your dog and leave him unsupervised. Heat is not as accessible as cold, but it is a great addition to your massage practice. Very useful in recovery treatment and in maintenance programs, heat is an easy and inexpensive way to tremendously improve your effectiveness. Acquire the necessary equipment and use it.

The use of water applications will greatly enhance your work and bring a lot of comfort to your animal. When well organized, they are a quick and inexpensive form of therapy to add to your massage routines.

6

PRINCIPLES AND CONCEPTS OF MASSAGE

Massages applied with knowledge and skill not only help specific health problems in dogs, but also improve their general health and fitness. Massage has a positive influence on both the physical and psychological well being of dogs of all ages and conditions. The caring feeling transmitted to a dog through the soothing contact of massage will contribute to the relaxation of the nervous system and assist in relieving its stress. The mechanical effect of massage on the body's tissues will increase blood circulation, improve the input of nutrients and fresh oxygen, as well as facilitate the removal of toxins and metabolic waste. It will loosen tight muscle fibers, knots, spasms and trigger points.

Massage has a profound overall effect on animals by influencing the body systems in the following ways:

- ❖ Stimulating or sedating the nervous system.

- ❖ Increasing or draining blood flow through the blood vascular system.

- ❖ Accelerating the cleansing effect of the lymph vascular system.

- ❖ Increasing oxygen/gas exchanges through the respiratory system.

- ❖ Increasing the metabolic rate of the digestive system.

- ❖ Increasing fluid circulation of the urinary system.

- ❖ Increasing nutrition and flexibility of the muscular system.

- ❖ Increasing nutrition of the bone and joint structure.

After a massage, the "feel good" sensation derived erases much nervous tension and anxiety. This sensation will convey a sense of satisfaction and reconnection with life that subconsciously promotes recovery and improvement.

During the first massage, your dog might wonder what you are doing, but after a few sessions he will show signs of enjoyment during the massage sessions (head down, eyes almost closed, ears relaxed). When dealing with painful conditions, massage therapy has a pain relief effect on the animal. Although unproven scientifically, it is theorized that massage inhibits

pain by stimulating the release of endorphins, which are opiate-like enzymes produced in the brain to reduce pain
awareness.

The Skills of Massage

In order to develop your skills in massage,
you need to understand, feel, and recognize
the various elements that are part of giving
a massage. The quality of your touch is
most important as it delivers a soothing
feeling to the dog and your touch will
perceive the structures being worked on as
well. In order to develop your skills in
massage, consider these factors.

Proper Approach

The way you approach your dog is most
important—for example, being calm and
aware of his personality. (See chapter 1 for
more details.) A full understanding of the
importance of the proper approach will
ensure good mental and physical contact
during a massage treatment.

Proper Posture

Your good posture is essential in giving a
good massage. Good posture and proper
table height (see chapter 1 for suggestions
for positioning your dog for massage)
help you save your energy by avoiding
unnecessary movement and reducing
fatigue.

Good posture is essential for the mechanical efficiency of the body. With good
posture, you will feel well grounded in
your work and more centered. You will

feel your own body's energy field as well
as your dog's, and this will allow a better
exchange between the two of you. With
your arms and hands relaxed, you will
perform the massage smoothly, avoiding
tension in your chest, shoulder and back
areas. As you get involved in the work,
take deep breaths regularly to keep
relaxed.

To maintain good posture, be sure to do
the following:

❖ Stand with your back straight, neither
  rigidly nor stiffly. Your shoulders
  should be loose and mobile.

❖ Relax and breathe slowly and
  deeply. Adapt your breathing
  rhythm to that of the dog.

❖ Keep your head straight. Imagine a
  cord pulling you up lightly from the
  top of your head to the ground.

❖ Tuck in your chin slightly.

❖ Look forward.

❖ Drop your shoulders. Do not tense
  your neck.

❖ Stretch out your arms, then let the
  elbows flex a little. You will now be
  at the proper distance from the dog.

❖ Develop a feeling of working from
  your elbows, not just your hands
  and wrists; this action will save
  energy and prevent soreness.
  Furthermore, it will give you more
  strength as you will feel more connected to your whole body.

❖ Use your body weight when doing
  large movements (for example,
  effleurage) to prevent serious fatigue.

❖ Bend your legs slightly at the knee, keeping your feet apart at shoulder width, similar to a Tai Chi stance.

❖ Be light on your feet to always be ready to move, using your full body weight in your movements. This agility also will help prevent awkward situations should the dog move unexpectedly.

❖ Work from your pelvis when exerting pressure; this action will help you exert more power from your body, saving tension in your arm and shoulder.

In summary, always be aware of your posture during a massage. You will maximize your energy and the quality of your treatment. With some practice, good posture will become automatic to you.

For proper posture to become second nature to you, practice mental reinforcement at the beginning of or during a treatment with the following "posture check":

❖ Head up, chin in, look forward.

❖ Back straight, not stiff, breathing relaxed.

❖ Neck relaxed, shoulders loose, elbows flexed.

❖ Knees slightly flexed, feet apart at shoulder width.

❖ Moving and flowing from the pelvis.

With your arms and hands relaxed, good posture will allow you to perform the massage smoothly and avoid tension in your chest, shoulders and back. As you get involved in the work, take deep breaths regularly to keep relaxed. Use your body weight to regulate the amount of pressure applied. Avoid unnecessary movements of the body that will fatigue you and may annoy the animal.

Good posture will ensure an energy flow from your hands to the dog and back to you, benefiting both you and the dog. Stand fairly close to your dog to reinforce this energy exchange. It is important to give the dog the feeling of closeness to increase his relaxation and benefit from your treatment. But exercise judgment. Closeness reinforces the feeling of care that occurs naturally when giving a massage, but if the dog objects to your proximity, you should always be ready to move away.

SENSITIVITY OF THE HANDS

A good touch provides a soothing and comforting feeling during your massage. The palms of your hands and your fingertips will give you accurate feedback on the physiological state of the various parts you are working on. However, learning to trust your hands is not easy. You must concentrate to detect subtle changes in the body on which you are working. The quality of your work depends strongly on the sensitivity of your hands.

In the early stages of your practice, a good way to develop your perception is to work with your eyes closed. This will help you focus on your fingertips, developing your tactility ("feel-see") and enhancing

6.1   Proper Posture, Standing

*6.2   **Proper Posture, Standing:** Back straight, elbows and knees flexed.*

6.3 *Proper   Posture,   Sitting:* *Comfortable   with   back straight, arm relaxed and elbow flexed.*

6.4 *Proper Posture, Sitting*

your "giving" touch awareness. This manual participation in the massage has a double beneficial effect for you. First, massage stimulates the circulation of blood to your hands and fingertips, nourishing them and preventing congestion. Second, because the nerves in the fingertips are directly connected to the brain, the use of the hands tends to promote a feeling of psychological ease. The Chinese habit of turning walnuts around and around in the hand springs from a knowledge of the salutary effect of manual activity.

THE FOUR T'S

The fingers' nerve endings will give you considerable information about the physiological state of the body part you are massaging. The sensations you perceive can be classified into four main categories: temperature, texture, tension and tenderness.

TEMPERATURE

The normal body temperature of a dog is 39°C (100 to 106°F). Changes in the temperature of the dog's skin suggest that a problem might exist. For example, an area that is abnormally cool to the touch (due to lack of blood circulation in that area) compared to the rest of the body, may indicate problems such as muscle contraction, deep chronic tension, and shock. An area that is hot to the touch indicates the presence of an inflammation and is a sure sign of an underlying problem such as a microspasm, stress point, trigger point, or trauma.

TEXTURE

Texture of the tissues refers to the density and the elasticity of the skin and muscular fibers. With practice on healthy animals, you will quickly develop a sense of touch for what normal, healthy tissues feel like. Tissues that feel either too soft or too puffy indicate the presence of swelling (edema), which is a sign of congestion or an underlying inflammatory condition.

TENDERNESS

Tenderness of the structures (muscles, tendons, ligaments, joints) refers to the sensitivity response of the animal to your touch (see chapter 1 for a description of feedback signs). If sensitivity is high, it is a sure sign of an underlying problem—nerve endings that are irritated or perhaps damaged. The dog's reaction to your touch is proportional to the degree of severity of that condition and of its stress level.

TENSION

Tension refers to the tonicity of the muscle fibers. Muscle tension is the result of too much exercise. Sometimes, muscle tension can result from scar tissue build-up (post-trauma). Too much tightness means less blood circulation, less nutrients and less oxygen. Tension will increase toxin buildup, creating an underlying inflammation. Trigger points (lactic acid build-ups) and stress points (small spasms) might result. It is normal to expect some high muscle tone immediately after exercise. However, finding tension in the muscle fibers after a good rest is a sure sign of a muscular compensation problem that often develops in response to some other problem. Too much tension in a muscle may be a sign of scar tissue developing as a result of an inflammation.

Thus, when you start a massage, always remember to use your fingers as sensors to get feedback through the four T's on the condition of the animal you are working on. Your fingers should become an extension of your brain. Use them as probes, quickly feeling and assessing what they touch, knowing almost instinctively how to adjust the pressure and to adapt to the right massage move. You will be amazed to find how fast this heightened perception will develop in you.

PRESSURE, CONTACT AND RHYTHM

The key to a successful massage is in the heightened perception of your fingers and the mastering of pressure, contact and rhythm.

PRESSURE

To appreciate how much pressure you are applying in a massage, experiment by pressing on a kitchen or a bathroom scale. You will be amazed to find how quickly pressure builds up. Practice by using simultaneously or alternately, one thumb, two thumbs, fingers of one hand, fingers of two hands, the palm of the hand, two palms, one fist, two fists, your elbow, and so on. Then practice the various massage moves (see chapter 7) on the scale with

and without using your body weight. Be creative! This exercise will help you realize how little exertion you need in order to reach deep into the muscle structure.

During a massage, be very careful of the pressure you exert. Too much pressure can bruise the muscle fibers without being noticed. Obviously, a bruise can't be seen under the dog's coat. The indication of a bruise will be the slight hardening of the tissues—caused by a congestion of blood —and the tenderness of the tissues that you will feel on palpation shortly after treatment.

Also use a weight scale to practice evaluating a 1 or 3 pound pressure, then a 5 or 10 pound and up to 15 or 20 pounds. Repeat the exercise until you are aware and can feel what it takes for you to reach any desired level of pressure.

A finger stroking touch rates at 0.1 to 0.5 pound. A light touch is 0.5 to 3 pounds. A regular touch is 3 to 5 pounds. A firm touch is 8 to 15 pounds. A heavy pressure starts at 15 pounds. More than 25 pounds pressure can bruise fibers in the muscle layers of an average animal. Use heavy pressure only on large muscle groups. If the dog has been well warmed-up, he will take the heavy pressure much more easily during the massage.

When working on scar tissue or on ligaments use up to 25 pounds pressure, but again be very careful at that particular stage of your massage. The best pressure is one sufficient to cause a sensation midway between pleasure and pain. A good masseur or masseuse can apply pressure that produces deep bodily effects without discomfort. When getting to the deeper aspects of your work, closely observe the animal's feedback signs, and especially the eyes.

Remember, your posture should always be such that you use your body weight at all times; if necessary, you can relieve the pressure immediately. Using your body's weight will prevent fatigue of your shoulder, neck and arms.

Choosing the right degree of pressure will mostly depend on the symptoms shown by the dog (for example, if an inflammation is present or not) and by your goals in this particular massage (whether it's for maintenance or to help relieve discomfort).

Always begin with light pressure and work progressively into heavier pressure. Never jab your fingers into the animal's flesh. Start with light strokings; follow with effleurages; then build up your work with wringings, kneadings or compressions, all interspersed with effleurages (every 20 to 30 seconds) before using pressures above the 15 pound mark. Do not get carried away while working over stress or trigger points or on scar tissue. Very heavy pressure will trigger soreness in the muscles, especially the next day. Use the 4 T's. Always pay attention to the feedback signs of the animal, and "listen" to your fingers. Pain and discomfort should always be regarded as warning signals. Be attentive, constantly adjusting the pressure of your massage. It's better to give several light massages than one that is too heavy. Consequently, always ease off progressively from heavier pressure work by using lighter wringings, general finger frictions, kneadings, and so on, all interspersed with effleurages every 20 to 30 seconds.

CONTACT

To get the best touch contact with the dog, keep your hands flexible, molding them to his body parts. Remember this is your point of contact with the animal. A mindful contact will be strongly perceived by the animal, strengthening his trust in your work. Much information passes through your hands, both to you and to the animal. You should feel a lot of warmth—and lots of energy—flowing through your hands during a massage. This deeper sense of contact will give you much feedback on what is happening with the animal as you are progressing with your massage.

Always weave each stroke into the other to give a feeling of continuity. Never remove your hands completely before the end of a massage move. At all times, keep hand contact even when going around the dog to go on the other side. If you do not weave your moves one into another or if you often loose hand contact during the massage, you will create a disruptive feeling that prevents the dog from relaxing (you would feel the same if you were being massaged in that manner). Keeping hand contact makes a big difference in ensuring connection and comfort. Your proper posture will ensure that you work smoothly, passing on a feeling of general relaxation to the animal.

Being continually in contact during a massage, your thumbs, your fingers and your palms need careful attention. Whether employing the thumbs or the

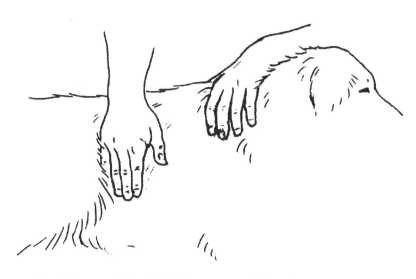

6.5   *Proper Hand Contact:* *Hands in full contact, molded to the part.*

fingers, always press downward using the bulbs of the tips, not just the tips. When pressing forward with the tips you can tire or even injure your hands. Overuse of finger joints can result in premature arthritis. Because living tissues develop with use, years of correct massage action can give you well developed, silky-smooth thumbs of the kind essential to this profession.

RHYTHM

In this context, rhythm refers to the frequency in which you apply your movements. Rhythm plays a strong factor in the effectiveness of your massage.

A gentle almost slow rhythm of 1 stroke per second is used most frequently. Use a soothing rhythm to start your session, to weave your moves into one another, and to finish your work. A soothing rhythm works wonders in relaxing the dog's nervous system, yet this soft approach allows you to work deeply if necessary. A faster rhythm stimulates the animal. It is used to perk up the animal before exercising, to stir up circulation before deep massage or simply to warm up your animal when it is chilled. Be aware that too brisk a rhythm could quickly irritate the dog, causing it to react against this type of massage. Always start with a gentle rhythm until you clue in on the comfortable rhythm for your dog. (The choice of specific rhythm is discussed in the various techniques and routines in chapters 8 and 9.) Develop your sense of rhythm by counting in your head, by listening to music or by singing.

With practice you will develop an inner appreciation of the feedback from your fingers and will know exactly how to adjust the right pressure with the right contact and at the right rhythm. Solid knowledge of the structure you are working on and of your massage techniques plus a strong dose of common sense are all you need to keep these three dimensions of pressure, contact and rhythm in harmony.

7

Massage has many positive effects; we describe the most important ones in this chapter.

Mechanical Effect

Mechanical effect is the actual physical contact caused by the pressure applied on the body. Therefore the mechanical effect is directly proportional to the pressure. The force you exert in the massage moves will stretch the tissues and drive the fluids (arterial, venous and lymphatic) in the direction of the movements. Light pressure will gently start things moving, whereas heavier pressure will strongly affect the area being worked on. Responding to the mechanical stimulation of the tissues, there is an increase in blood circulation in the area massaged. The results are better tissue oxygenation, better metabolism, and lowered blood pressure. Deep mechanical pressure will also contribute to the release of endorphins. Although unproven scientifically, it is theorized that massage inhibits pain by stimulating endorphin release. The mechanical pressure of specific massage

moves will stretch and soften the tissues. This stretching and softening will help release muscle tension, contractures, trigger points, stress points and spasms, eventually breaking down restrictive collagen fibers (scar tissue).

Mechanical pressure also produces an effect on the nervous system. Depending on the type of application, it will either stimulate or soothe muscles. For example, slow, rhythmic, light-to-medium pressure will soothe and relax very efficiently, whereas faster rhythm with medium-to-heavy pressure will stimulate very quickly.

Pure Nervous Reflex Effect

The pure nervous reflex effect refers to the class of movement that influences only the nervous system (see chapter 2). This nervous reflex effect is achieved with a very light touch. Exert almost no pressure, but rather lightly contact the skin to touch the cutaneous (skin) sensory nerve endings. Stroking, fine vibrations, and very light and slow effleurage are mostly used to elicit this nervous reflex effect. Gentle stimulation of the dermatomes (skin sensory nerve endings) sends relaxing impulses to the brain. The motor nerves, which are responsible for muscular contractions or nervous anxiety, then let go of the tension. For this type of massage, use a slow, gentle, soothing and nourishing rhythm of 1 stroke per second or slower on average.

Pure nervous reflex is used primarily to soothe and relax when you need to calm your animal in a state of general tension, anxiety, shock or pain (see the relaxation massage routine in chapter 9). Pure nervous reflex does not increase the secretion of glands, cause a chemical effect, or have a mechanical impact on circulation of fluids.

MASSAGE MOVES

This section introduces the seven essential classes of massage moves and a multitude of combinations. The seven essential classes of massage moves are stroking, effleurage, petrissage, shaking, vibration, friction and tapotements.

Each individual class contains several moves and each move can be performed in either a soothing or a stimulating manner, depending on the pressure and the rhythm applied. As a rule, the rhythm of application should be 20 strokes per minute for a slow rhythm, 60 strokes per minute (1 per second) for a gentle rhythm, 80–90 strokes per minute for a faster, stimulating rhythm. Indeed, the size of the area you massage influences the adjustment of your rhythm (for example,

when stroking a long back versus stroking short legs). Finer adjustments are specified with each class and movement.

Some of the movements appear very similar, but they all offer specifics of which you need to be aware. This knowledge will help you become an expert in choosing the right massage move to suit the purpose of the massage. With practice this will become second nature to you. Remember that each massage movement helps you "feel" the structures you work on and therefore gives you tremendous feedback. Due to the high sensitivity of your dog, always start lightly before increasing pressure or rhythm.

STROKING

Stroking is used for its soothing, relaxing and calming effect (pure nervous reflex effect) on the body, directly affecting the central nervous system. It is the main move used in the relaxation massage routine. When the dog is very nervous, stroking his back and legs will soothe and "ground" him.

You always start and finish a massage routine by applying several strokings over the body part that has been worked on. Also use strokings to weave various massage techniques or when moving from one area of the body to another.

Stroking movements are performed in a relaxed, superficial manner with the tips of the fingers or the palms of the hands, very lightly. When stroking, use very light pressure, from 0.1 to 0.5 pound pressure. This is a pure nervous reflex move, so there is no need for mechanical pressure. Stroking can be done in any direction, but preferably along the length of the muscles, following the direction in which the hair lies.

Done in slow motion (10 to 20 strokes per minute, 1 stroke every 3 to 6 seconds on average), stroking gives a very soothing, relaxing sensation that is almost sedative in its effect. Done faster (1 to 2 stroke

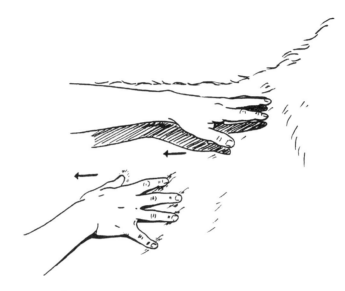

7.1   Stroking Massage Movement

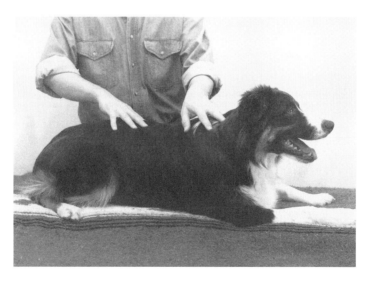

7.2   Stroking Massage Movement

every second), stroking will have a stimulating, almost exciting effect on the animal's nervous system.

EFFLEURAGE

Effleurage is the move you will use the most. Effleurage is used as every second move (every 10–20 seconds) during most of the massage work to emphasize proper drainage. After strokings, it is used to start, weave or terminate any massage routine or technique. To assist the natural flow of the venous blood circulation, always perform effleurage toward the heart.

Effleurage is a gliding movement done with the palmar aspect of the whole hand (fingers and palm). During an

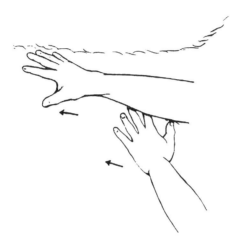

7.3   Effleurage Massage Movement

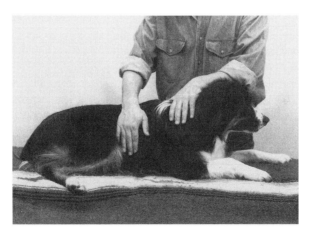

7.4   Effleurage Massage Movement

effleurage stroke, the thumb never leads the hand, but rather it follows the fingers. The hand should be well-molded and in full contact with the body part being massaged. You can use one or two hands, simultaneously or alternately, in an even gliding movement. The pressure is usually even throughout the entire stroke, except, for example, when going over bony processes such as the scapular ridge, point of the hip, or point of the elbow or hock.

Effleurage has a mechanical, draining effect on body fluids such as blood and lymph. This draining effect is proportional to the pressure applied and the rhythm of the movement. The rhythm of your effleurages should be smooth, 20 strokes per minute on average (1 stroke every 2 or 3 seconds). A faster rhythm, 1 or 2 strokes per second is more invigorating.

When performed in a superficial manner with a light pressure (2 or 3 pounds) and a slow rhythm (1 stroke per 2 or 3 seconds on average), effleurage will have a very soothing effect in addition to boosting the circulation. Due to the comforting feeling it gives, this massage move is very good when starting or finishing a massage.

When effleurage is done in a similar fashion but with a faster rhythm (2 strokes per second), it is more stimulating. It can be used in this way during massage on small areas to drain swelling without hurting the structure, but do not use this combination over a large area. The fast rhythm often causes nerve irritation and makes the dog nervous.

When effleurage is applied in a deep manner with heavy pressure (10 or 15 pounds) and a slow rhythm, it stimulates the body by increasing blood and lymph circulation. Yet the slow rhythm still soothes the nervous system. This combination is used to drain large areas between sequences of massage moves as in the maintenance massage routine and the recuperation routine after heavy training (see chapter 9 for more on both routines).

When effleurage is done in a deep manner with faster rhythm, it strongly stimulates the circulation. In this fashion, effleurage is used mostly to perk up the muscles just before exercise or as a warm-up move at the end of a maintenance massage routine.

When doing effleurage on a narrow area, (for example, the lower legs) use mostly the palmar region of the fingers instead of the whole hand. Adjust the pressure corresponding to the structure being worked on. Work lightly over ligaments and bony structures but more heavily over muscle groups.

Always perform effleurage toward the heart to assist the natural flow of the venous blood circulation.

PETRISSAGE

Petrissage is the foundation of massage. It comprises kneading, compression, muscle squeezing, wringing up and skin rolling.

All these moves are mechanical and soothing (rhythm of 1 stroke per second), but if done quickly (2 to 4 strokes per second), they will become stimulating. The moves are intended to clean tissues of waste products and to assist circulatory interchange.

Petrissage manipulations are done with pressure and relaxation alternately. With the kneading, compression and muscle squeezing massage moves, the tissues are pressed against the underlying structure. While with the wringing up and skin rolling massage moves, the tissues are lifted away from the underlying structure. Used constantly in sport massage, these moves work on muscle tension, muscle knots, congestion and small spasms.

KNEADING

Kneading is a very effective technique performed with the thumbs or the palmar

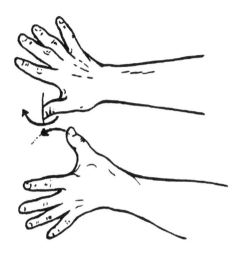

7.5 Petrissage Class of Movement: *Double Thumb Kneading*

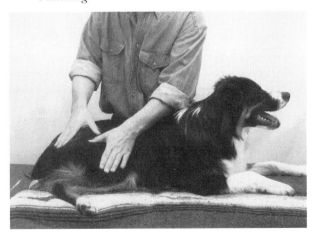

7.6 Petrissage Class of Movement: *Double Thumb Kneading*

surface of the three fingertips (index, major and ring finger). It is done in a rhythmical, circular way (small half circles overlapping one another, pushing outward) the same way you would knead dough. Contact is maintained at all times.

The tissues are intermittently compressed against the underlying bone structure. In a relaxing mode, the rhythm should be 1 movement per second; to stimulate, increase the rate to 2 to 4 movements per second. Kneading will have a pumping effect that boosts the circulation, improves the oxygenation and helps remove toxins from the tissues. It gives in-depth touch to the various bundles of muscle fibers, separating them, draining them and cleansing them from toxin buildup. Kneading will help you feel scar tissue patches or small spasms (stress points).

Kneading is usually performed with two hands, but it may be performed with one hand when the area treated is small (the flexor tendon, for example). You can try other combinations using only two fingers or a thumb and fingers. When dealing with large areas (the hind legs, for example), use the palms of your hands in combination with your body weight (proper posture). It is a very efficient technique.

When kneading, gauge your pressure. Start at 2 or 3 pounds. Increase to between 5 and 12 pounds when working the big bulky muscle groups on larger dogs. Intersperse your kneadings with a good deal of effleurages every 20 seconds.

COMPRESSION

Compression movements are made with the palm of the hand or with a lightly clenched fist, alternating each hand rhythmically and applying pressure directly onto the muscle groups. Compression is applicable to large dogs only when working over large, bulky muscle areas such as the hind legs. The method is similar to kneadings but without the gliding movement over the muscles. The rhythm should be of 1 compression every second. Any faster would be highly stimulating, almost irritating to most animal. Do not use compression on bony or thin muscle layered areas.

Compression complements kneading; it is used to save time and reduce fatigue when working on large muscle groups. Compression produces the same pumping effect and offers the same benefits as does kneading. Be careful not to over-compress the muscles. Gauge your pressure at between 10 and 20 pounds maximum. It is better to repeat the exercise several times and secure the desired effect than to go too fast or too heavily resulting in irritated or bruised fibers. Intersperse your compressions with a good deal of effleurages every 10 to 20 seconds.

MUSCLE SQUEEZING

Muscle squeezing is mostly used to decongest and relax tense muscles. It is used mostly along the crest of the neck and is a very useful move to work on the legs and the tail. The movement is made between extended fingers and the heal of the hand using the entire palm surface in full contact with the body part. You can

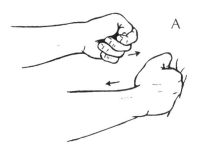 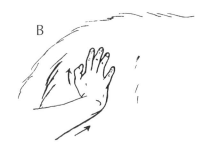

7.7   Petrissage Class of Movement: *Compression*

(A) Fist Compression
(B) Palmar Compression

7.8   Petrissage Class of Movement: *Palmar Compression*

7.9   Petrissage Class of Movement: *Fist Compression*

use one hand or two hands to deliver muscle squeezings. Taking care not to pull the muscle away from its bony support, grasp and gently squeeze it.

Muscle squeezing accomplishes several things. It gives a strong feel of touch to the animal and therefore deepens the relaxation of the muscle. It gives you feedback about the tension in these particular fibers. And it has a pumping effect on both the blood and lymph circulation.

Because we only want to relax and decongest, it is not necessary to exert a lot of pressure in this move. When muscle

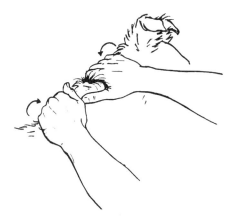

7.10 *Petrissage Class of Movement:* Muscle Squeezing

7.11 *Petrissage Class of Movement:* Double Hand Muscle Squeezing

squeezing, always start gently with 5 to 10 pounds pressure. You can use 15 pounds pressure if dealing with bulkier muscle groups of larger dogs (thicker neck, legs or pectoral muscles). But remember, if there is tenderness in the muscle, squeeze very gently.

Using muscle squeezing in a soothing, slow rhythm (1 squeeze every second) has a strong calming effect on the nervous system. It is used for this purpose in the relaxing massage routine over the neck. When done in a brisk manner (2 to 4 squeezes per second), double hands muscle squeezing has a very stimulating effect both on the circulation and on the nervous system. The fast pace invigorates the animal. It is a very useful move to warm up the leg muscles such as the triceps, the flexors and extensors of the legs during cold weather.

WRINGING UP

Wringing up is a great move to use on the back of the dog, the shoulders and hindquarters. Wringing up efficiently increases the circulation, improves the oxygenation and removes toxins. It is very useful in reducing inflammation over the muscles of the back—and dogs love it!

Wringing up is done with the palms, thumbs abducted at a 90° angle. Apply both hands flat on the body part, and then start wringing the muscle side to side, almost in the same way you would wring wet linens. The muscle is lightly and gently lifted then wrung side-to-side.

Wringing up is very efficient in stimulating the circulation and warming up muscle groups in a short time. Wringing up can be applied anywhere on the dog's body. Use an average pressure, starting at about 2 pounds and building up to 15 pounds depending on the muscle mass worked on. Remain light when going over bony areas such as the spine, the scapula or point of the hip. Your rhythm should be smooth and 1 stroke per second or less on average. A faster rhythm of 2 strokes per second will be very stimulating and may be irritating to the dog.

SKIN ROLLING

Skin rolling is a very soothing manipulation that is used mostly to keep the dermal layer rich in blood. Skin rolling is used mostly to maintain a healthy and shiny coat, break down little fatty deposits, prevent the formation of excess adhesions and maintain good elasticity of the skin.

With thumbs on one side and fingers on the other, grasp and lift the tissues. Using either one or both hands (preferably both), push the thumbs forward rolling the skin toward the fingers. The fingers draw the skin toward the thumbs, lifting, stretching and squeezing the tissues.

Skin rolling is a gliding motion of the superficial tissues (skin and fat). It should be performed in a slow, soothing manner to avoid irritating the skin nerve endings, especially over areas where the tissues lie tight on the underlying structures. The angle of direction may be varied and repeated to ensure maximum effect to the tissues. This is a great technique to enhance nerve and blood circulation. Use only 2 or 3 pounds pressure maximum!

VIBRATIONS

This interesting manipulation is mostly used to reach below superficial tissues into the deeper structures of muscles or joints. It is a quivering type of movement done with the hand. It has a soothing effect and can be used alone or inserted into a routine or treatment.

At the start, use no pressure other than the weight of your hand on the part to be vibrated (0.5 pound maximum). Progressively increase your pressure by a few pounds to the point of stretching the structure you are treating. Start the vibration movements from the elbow and translate them through your wrist to your hand, this is known as a "flat hand vibration."

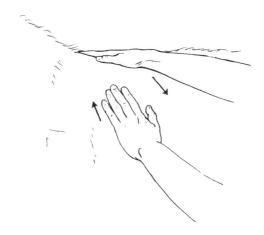

7.12   Petrissage Class of Movement: Wringing

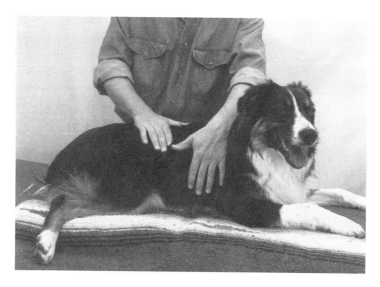

7.13   Petrissage Class of Movement: Wringing

You can use another variation called the "point vibration." This is done with the thumb or the fingertips only, giving you more accuracy for small specific areas. The aim is to pass a soothing vibration to the tissues deep under the skin.

Done gently with 1 or 2 pounds of pressure and applied with a fine, gentle rhythm, vibrations have a mechanical soothing effect with a strong nervous reflex effect. Applied with 3 to 5 pounds of pressure and a faster, more aggressive

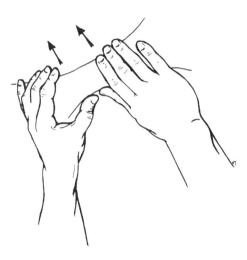

7.14 Petrissage Class of Movement: *Skin Rolling*

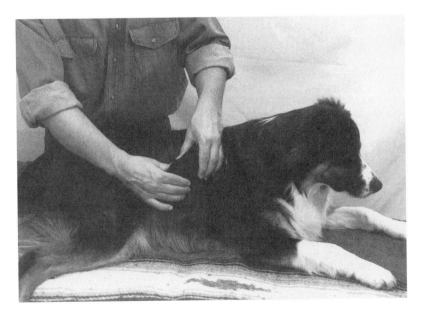

7.15 Petrissage Class of Movement: *Skin Rolling*

vibrational rhythm, vibrations are a mechanically stimulating move and less of a nervous reflex.

This manipulation is very useful in relaxing the nervous system. Use the flat hand vibration move in a gentle manner (light pressure) over the sacrum for a few minutes when starting the relaxation routine. It is very efficient in eliciting the parasympathetic nervous response (see chapter 2). It is not recommended to use this move directly over the head (skull). Apply vibration to joints and around

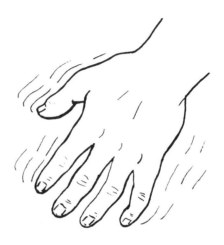

7.16   Vibration Massage Movement

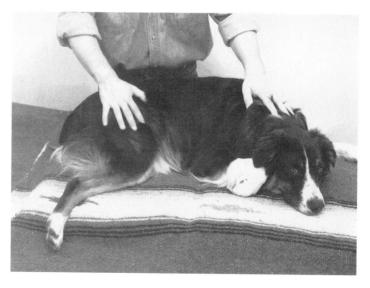

7.17   Vibration Massage Movement

bony prominences. It soothes swollen joints both in the cases of acute trauma and chronic injury. Vibrations are also good for inflamed rheumatism or arthritis where regular massage is contraindicated. Use vibrations near well-healed scar tissue to reduce adhesions. Depending on the area, apply no more than 5 to 10 pounds pressure until the animal's maximum tolerance is reached.

Start with a small vibratory movement, maintaining it for a few seconds, then gradually release and move to another position. Start again and repeat over the whole area you want to treat. Intersperse effleurage and stroking frequently with this move to drain the tissues and relax the animal.

SHAKING

Shaking is a very strong mechanical movement used frequently in sport massage to stimulate circulation. Shaking is performed either by the fingertips or with the whole palm of the hand in full contact with the body part. The skin is shaken over the muscle structure. It can either be a short shaking over a small area or a large shaking over a larger area.

When done in a gentle manner (1 stroke per second), shaking is soothing. When applied briskly (2 or 3 strokes per second), it is one of the most stimulating massage moves.

Pressure should be kept between 3 and 5 pounds. The skin can move with your hands over the body parts. When working more coarsely (heavier pressure, faster rhythm), the hands glide over the skin. As

you work in this manner, pay attention to the animal's feedback signs. Take care not to irritate the nerve endings of the skin, especially if an inflammation is present. Adjust your rhythm and pressure accordingly. Always ease off a little when going over bony processes such as the point of the hip or the scapular spine. A full treatment of this move alone should not exceed 3 to 5 minutes depending on the size of the dog.

FRICTION

This very specific movement is mostly used in sport therapy to break down adhesions developing over muscular fibers, tendons, ligaments and fascia. Always warm up the area thoroughly with effleurages, wringing up and kneadings before proceeding to frictions.

Frictions consist of small, deep movements applied across the length of the muscle fiber bundle or up and down over a patch of fibrous tissue. Use the tip of your thumb or first three fingers to friction small, local areas. Use both hands to friction large areas. With any of these friction movements, expect to see a lot of loose fur being removed.

Friction can be done gently or coarsely depending on your aim. Both styles are mechanically stimulating to the body, causing a very strong hyperaemia response (increased blood circulation). Keep in mind the degree of tissue inflammation present (if any), the dimension of the adhesions and their location in relation to other structures—is it close to a bone, joint, nerve or vein?

To break down fibrous adhesions, you need to use a fair amount of pressure, starting around 10 to 12 pounds pressure, progressively building up to a maximum of 20 pounds. Always warm up the area thoroughly before starting. Your rhythm can be of 1 or 2 strokes per second for slow frictions, and up to 4 frictions per second for fast frictions. When using the heavier pressure, always keep the friction movements smooth and fast. Do not use friction on any one specific area for too long. At any given time, 2 to 3 minutes is enough up to a maximum of 4 or 5

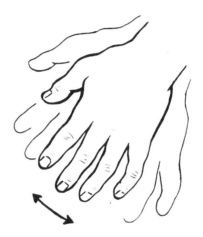

7.18 *Shaking Massage Movement*

7.19 *Shaking Massage Movement*

minutes if no inflammation is present. It is better to reduce scar formation over the course of several massages than to take the risk of worsening the area by overworking it and creating more inflammation. It is very important to intersperse your work with copious drainage every 10 to 20 seconds and some wringing up to keep the tissues warm.

When working a patch of scar tissue, start from the periphery toward the center of the scar with fairly low pressure (8 to 12 pounds) to loosen the fibers. Drain

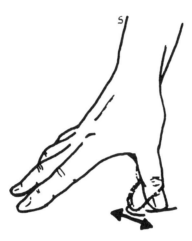

7.20   *Thumb Friction Movement*

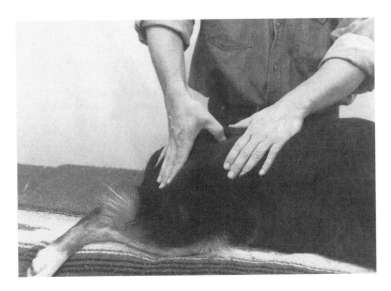

7.21   *Thumb Friction Movement*

thoroughly with effleurages, and then use friction across the whole fibrous patch, going sideways or up and down depending on the nature of the scar formation. Follow this with a circular motion using a much heavier pressure (15 to 20 pounds).

Assess the feedback signs of the dog. Remember to drain generously with effleurages every 20 seconds.

As you use friction to relieve new adhesions or to breakdown old ones, it is good

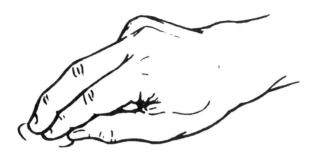

7.22   Finger Friction Movement

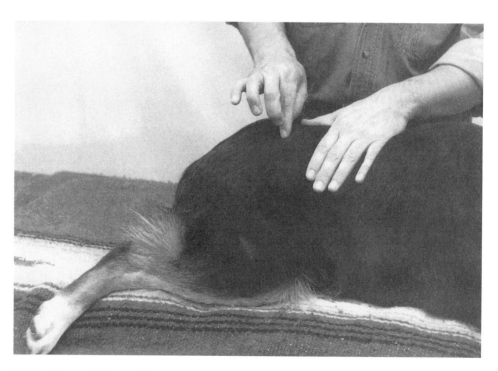

7.23   Finger Friction Movement

to ice before and after treatment. This will ensure the numbing of the nerve endings and will therefore keep the pain down. Simply apply a cold pack or use the ice massage technique described in chapter 5.

TAPOTEMENTS

Tapotement massage consists of a series of soft blows to the body done rhythmically. Tapotements comprise clapping, cupping, hacking and beating. All these movements are mechanical and stimulating. Hands

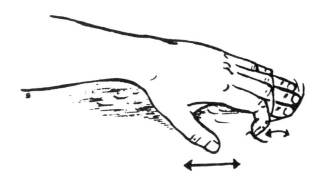

7.24   Hand Friction Movement

7.25   Double Hand Friction Movement

usually work alternately in a light and springy manner.

The rhythm of application varies according to the pressure. Light clapping, cupping and hacking are done at approximately 2 to 3 beats per second for starters, and up to 5 beats per second when warm. The heavier beating and pounding movements are performed more slowly at 2 to 3 beats per second. The moves are mostly used to stir up circulation, to stimulate the release of histamine and to energize the body; they are used frequently in therapeutic massage treatments, sport massage sessions and warm-up routines.

Done on their own, tapotements are very effective for warming up muscle groups just prior to exercise. Your dog might take some time to adapt to tapotements, but he will soon learn to like them. Start with a very light pressure, increasing progressively. The application of tapotements should last a few minutes: 30 seconds to 1 minute over small areas, up to 2 minutes when working large parts. A strong, soothing feeling of relaxation will follow such an application. Try it on yourself and you will see. Always finish with some effleurages and strokings.

CLAPPING

Clapping is done with the palm of the hand with the hand flat and the fingers stretched as though applauding.

Use only 2 or 3 pounds to start, building up to 5 or 10 pounds pressure. Use only on muscle groups, not on bony structures except over the rib cage. Keep the pressure light over thin muscles like the scapular muscles.

CUPPING

Cupping is done with the palm of the hand cupped as though holding water.

Use 5 pounds pressure. This is a softer version of clapping, mostly for adapting your hands around bony structures like the scapula and hip areas, or curved muscle areas like the front chest or rump.

HACKING

Hacking is done in a springing manner with the medial border of the hand and the fingers spread out in a flexible and non-rigid manner.

Use 5 to 8 pounds of pressure and up to 12 pounds when working over big bulky muscles. Hacking penetrates deeper into the muscle structure and yet is very gentle. It is a favorite move to treat the back muscles (longissimus dorsi, iliocostalis dorsi) or the thicker muscle of the hindquarters.

BEATING

Beating is done with a relaxed fist, hitting the muscle groups with the ulnar (or medial) side of the hand.

Pressure can be of 10 to 15 pounds and up to 20 pounds over big muscle groups. Only use this move after you have already done several clapping, cupping and hacking moves. This move is rarely used except for deep stimulation of big muscle groups like the hindquarters on big dogs. A strong stimulation of fluid circulation will immediately follow this application.

THE LAYING ON OF HANDS

The laying on of hands has great therapeutic value in soothing acute wounds,
inflammation, nerve irritation and stress of
mechanical or nervous origin.. The laying
on of hands is not considered a technical
massage movement in most traditional
massage manuals, but it is the oldest form
of massage. The technique is mostly used
when regular massage cannot be used; it is
a great addition to regular treatment routines and furthers the soothing effect.

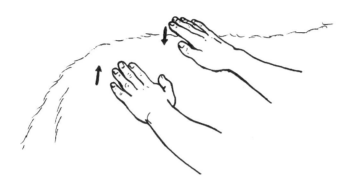

7.26   Tapotement: *Clapping Movement*

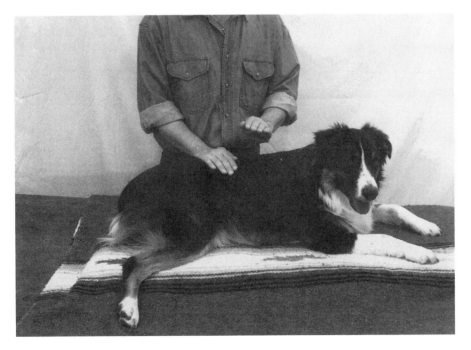

7.27   Tapotement: *Clapping Movement*

Put your hands gently over the area of concern and mindfully feel the energy and the warmth of that part. Use very little pressure (0.5 to 1 pound) for this simple hand contact. Be thoughtful of the moment, of the animal and of yourself as you do this. The feeling of closeness that will quickly develop between you and the animal is a sure sign of the effectiveness of this procedure. A warm feeling will develop between your hands. As the nervous stress connected to that particular

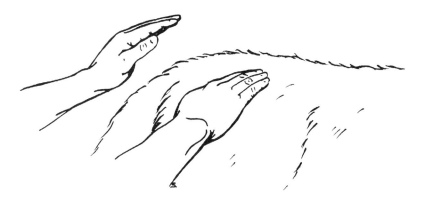

7.28   Tapotement: *Cupping Movement*

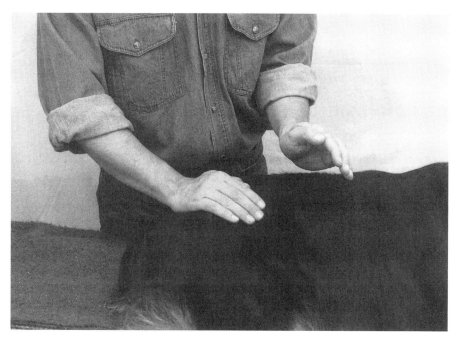

7.29   Tapotement: *Cupping Movement*

area is released, you will feel a heat wave coming out of the treated area. That heat wave will be proportional to the stress recorded and the pain involved. The laying on of hands will soothe the area and induce relaxation both on the physiological and the nervous levels. A great feeling of relief will follow such a procedure.

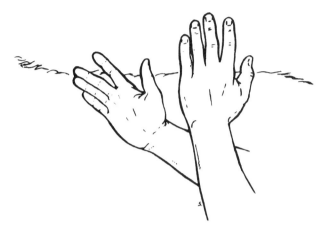

7.30   Tapotement: *Hacking Movement*

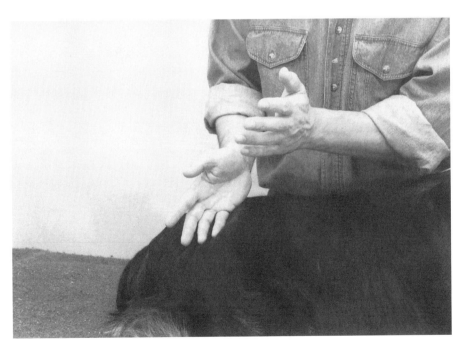

7.31   Tapotement: *Hacking Movement*

When massage is contraindicated, the laying on of hands will often bring soothing energy to an irritated area, relieving pain. It is recommended that you rinse your hands with fresh water after such treatment, to drain the "off" energy you picked up. Cold hydrotherapy (such as a simple cotton towel wrung out of cold

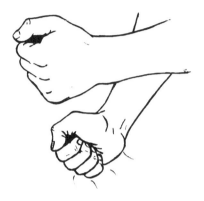

7.32   Tapotement: *Beating (medium pressure) and Pounding (heavy pressure) Movements*

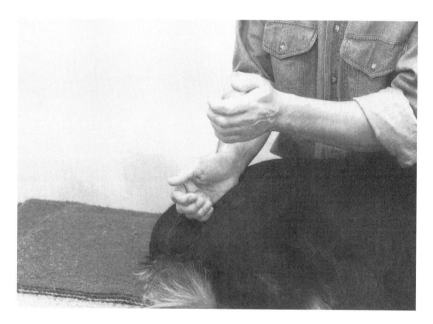

7.33   Tapotement: *Beating and Pounding Movements*

water as described in chapter 5) applied onto the animal's treated body part will also relieve the inflammation and pain considerably. The laying on of hands will definitely comfort your animal and assist his recovery.

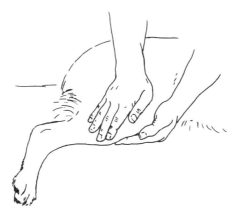

7.34 Laying On of Hands

7.35 Laying On of Hands

BASIC CLASSIFICATION OF MASSAGE MOVEMENTS

Massage is classified into three basic groups: soothing, stimulating and pure nervous reflex.

SOOTHING MASSAGE MOVEMENTS

The main characteristic of a soothing massage is its ability to inhibit nerve impulses to the muscles soothing them into relaxation. The soothing massage moves are as follows:

❖ Slow stroking.

❖ Gentle wringing.

❖ Gentle effleurage.

❖ Fine vibration.

❖ Fine shaking.

❖ Gentle petrissage with kneading, muscle squeezing, wringing up and eventually gentle compressions—all done with very light pressure and a peaceful rhythm.

STIMULATING MASSAGE MOVEMENTS

The main characteristic of a stimulating massage is that it causes a nerve exciting reflex in the muscles. This reflex stimulates muscle tone (light contraction) causing an increase in blood and lymph circulation with resultant increased oxygenation, improved nutrient intake and better removal of toxins and metabolic waste.

Rhythm and pressure play important roles in the degree of stimulation you want to induce. Working in a hasty manner with a fast rhythm and abrupt changes of movement will irritate your animal very quickly. Therefore, always start gently and build up your pressure and rhythm accordingly. Always pay attention to the feedback signs of the animal. Pressure need not be heavy. On a healthy structure, 10 to 20 pounds is plenty. The mechanical repetition of the movements will secure the effects desired. Always start lightly and monitor the feedback signs of your animal, adjusting accordingly.

In time—and with practice—you will develop a sense for the amount of pressure and the appropriate rhythm. You should always stay on the safe side by starting gently. As your dog becomes accustomed to the massage, he will allow you to work deeper especially he it is well warmed up. Always remember to ensure thorough drainage (effleurage) after using stimulating moves.

The stimulating moves are as follows:

❖ Fast stroking.

❖ Firm to vigorous effleurage.

❖ Petrissage with firm kneadings, compressions, wringing up and skin-rolling.

❖ Coarse vibrations.

❖ Coarse shaking.

❖ Frictions, fine and coarse.

❖ Tapotements with clapping, cupping, hacking and beating.

PURE NERVOUS REFLEX MOVEMENTS

The main characteristics of pure nervous reflex massage moves are that they induce reflex effects on the central nervous system (brain) and result in a "letting go" of nervous tension, stress and anxiety. Pure nervous reflex promotes strong relaxation.

The pure nervous reflex moves are as follows:

❖ Stroking.

❖ Very gentle effleurage.

❖ Fine vibrations.

❖ Laying of hands.

It is strongly recommended that you wash your hands with fresh water immediately after any massage work. Washing helps you unload all undesired residual energy picked up during the massage and avoids passing it on to other persons or animals. It will also center your vital energy before further activity.

Regular practice of massage on your dog will quickly develop your ability to feel the right approach for each type of massage. The enhanced perception of your fingertips will surprise you tremendously. You will be amazed at how much information you pick up and this, in turn, will help you appreciate the situation at hand. Remember, practice makes perfect. And even more, quality practice makes perfect!

8

MASSAGE TECHNIQUES

Massage techniques refer to specific massage moves arranged in a pattern and done in an orderly fashion to achieve a desired effect. These techniques can be applied to any body part and at any given time after proper warm-up of the structures to be worked on, unless massage is contraindicated (see chapter 1).

The massage techniques in this chapter have been developed to further your knowledge and to provide you with guidelines for the best course of massage in dealing with muscular problems. These techniques will prevent aggravation of those problems, speed up the healing process and ensure proper recovery.

Massage therapy has developed several deep massage techniques to eliminate muscle tightening and prevent toxin buildups. Muscle tightening causes muscle resistance to the natural motion of the body parts (for example, a shorter stride or restricted neck movement). It will lead to the buildup of stress points (small spasms), trigger points (lactic acid buildup), and

congestion of fluid circulation, which in turn will cause pain and potential lameness in the dog.

These techniques are as follows:

- ❖ The SEW/WES technique to start and finish any massage work.
- ❖ The thumb technique for a variety of effects.
- ❖ The swelling technique to deal with edema.
- ❖ The trigger point technique to deal with lactic acid buildup.
- ❖ The stress point technique to deal with small spasms.
- ❖ The origin/insertion technique to deal with chronic muscle contracture and full muscle spasms.

These techniques can be used separately or in any combination to ensure efficient overall treatment and positive results. Though we often use the swelling and origin/ insertion techniques in emergencies, all are used in maintenance and preventive routines according to the dog's level of play or training.

Here, more than anywhere else, the four T's apply—temperature, tension, texture and tenderness (see chapter 6). Every stroke will give you feedback on the condition under your fingertips. So listen to your fingers and adjust accordingly.

THE SEW/WES TECHNIQUE

This technique is very important in massage work. It gives you the proper approach for warming-up and for draining any area you wish to work on. The title of this technique is made up of two acronyms. The acronym SEW stands for Stroking, Effleurage and Wringing; the acronym WES stands for Wringing, Effleurage and Stroking.

The SEW approach is used to start and progressively warm up any area you are to massage. Always start with very light and gentle strokings over the area you will be massaging. Then follow with 2 to 3 effleurage passes to thoroughly cover the entire area all along draining toward the heart. Now apply gentle wringings (2 passes back and forth) over the whole area. Follow with a set of effleurages and continue with either kneadings, muscle squeezing or gentle friction depending on the nature of the massage you want to give. Remember to intersperse with effleurages every 20 seconds.

The WES approach is used when you are finished with the deeper aspect of the massage. This approach will allow you to properly and progressively move out of the area you worked on, ensuring proper drainage. After the last set of effleurages, following your deeper massage work, apply a gentle but firm set of wringings over the entire area worked on (2 passes back and forth). Follow with extra effleurages (twice as many as usual, 4 to 6 passes) to thoroughly drain the tissues you have massaged. With each effleurage passe you should release your pressure a little, starting around 6 pounds and ending with 3 pounds. Finish with a light stroking, covering the entire area.

The last bit of stroking in the WES approach can become the opening stroking of the SEW approach to the area you will massage next.

THE THUMB TECHNIQUE

The thumb technique plays a very important role in massage movements, in palpations and in assessing the structures to be treated. Due to its shape, strength and versatility, the thumb is a key player in most of your massage moves. It is your most valuable tool for deep work (friction of adhesions).

When using the thumb, form a 90° angle between it and the spread fingers. You can use the tip of the thumb like a probe or you can use the tip's medial or lateral aspects to make contact with angled surfaces.

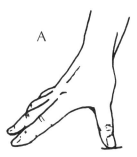

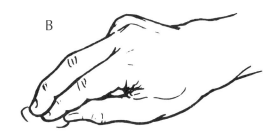

8.1   Thumb Technique

(A) Thumb Technique
(B) Reinforced Index Finger Technique

The thumb technique is very useful when performing specific and localized work. Never use the thumb without warming up the area treated (strokings, effleurages, kneadings, and so on). For more general, less localized, less specific work, you can use the broader surface of the thumb's last phalange. The thumb's extreme malleability allows you to modify the direction of your movement as well as the force you are using at any moment depending on the signs and symptoms of the area being treated. Thus, a wide range of therapeutic effects are possible. You can use the thumb to drain small or localized areas, stretch fibers, friction scar tissue, release trigger points and make investigative palpations and assessments. The thumb is not to be used mechanically across the tissues; it is to be applied intelligently with knowledge of the structures being treated.

Because of its highly developed nervous sensory endings, your thumb sends messages directly to your brain. If you close your eyes during thumb palpations, or indeed during any other work, you will feel minute changes in the tissues.

To maximize your strength when using the thumb during frictions or when applying deep pressure, use your body weight. You should feel the force going in a straight line from the shoulder, through the elbow, the thumb and to the target. Allow the elbow or the wrist to bend only a few degrees. Proper posture will facilitate your work and save your energy. The level of pressure used with the thumb depends on the pathological condition of the tissues treated, the nature of the work and the location of the treatment. Use your judgement, but remember that over 25 pound pressure may cause bruising in muscular tissues.

If your thumb is not strong enough, you can resort to using your index finger, reinforced with your thumb and middle finger (see figure 8.1B) following the same procedure as the thumb technique.

THE SWELLING TECHNIQUE

This technique is used to reduce edema (swelling) resulting from either acute or chronic injuries. A trauma such as a strain, sprain, wound, inflammation from over-work or the flare up of an old injury will cause an increased amount of fluid (lymph or blood) to the area that results in swelling. This increased volume of fluid will cause an increased tension of the tissues and skin rendering them very tender to the touch. The temperature of the swollen area will be higher than normal and proportional to the degree of inflammation. Remember that any acute phase of trauma is contraindicated to massage and that you should contact your veterinarian to ensure no other tissue damage is involved. When massage is contraindicated, use cold hydrotherapy instead until the initial swelling goes down, and then apply this massage technique.

The swelling technique should be preceded by the application of hydrotherapy as described in chapter 5—cold in acute cases, vascular flush (hot/cold) in sub-acute cases and heat in chronic cases. Choose the most practical device (ice packs, ice cup) available to you and apply it before your massage to induce a vaso-constriction of the tissues and numbing effect of the nerve endings. The ice cup massage is a terrific, practical technique to use with swellings.

Start with some light stroking moves over the body to relax the animal and help him accept your working close to the problem site; then apply your light strokings over the swollen area to soothe the irritated nerve endings. Your rhythm should be smooth at the rate of 1 stroke per second. Assess the feedback signs of your dog at all times. If the area appears very irritated, use the laying on of hands approach (see

chapter 7) or cold hydrotherapy (see chapter 5) before proceeding.

When the initial tenderness seems to be relieved, you can use a fine vibration movement to stimulate the circulation, then resume the light strokings. Weave your stroke into a very light effleurage—a maximum of 2 or 3 pounds pressure to avoid mechanical stress on the skin and deeper tissues—around the periphery of the swollen area, draining toward the heart. This will stimulate the circulation and begin the drainage process. Keep a relaxed pace of 1 move per second.

Next proceed with a very gentle double-thumb kneading massage at the edge of the swelling and go around the damaged area in a clockwise manner. Drain the excess fluid toward the outside of the swollen area, "shaving" half to 1 inch from the periphery. Always start on the outside, not at the center. Use 3 to 5 pounds pressure or less if the skin is very tight or tender. Even when light pressure is used, the mechanical effect will be sufficient to rapidly induce drainage. Keep assessing your dog's feedback and speak soothing words as you proceed.

After you have completed the first circumference around the swollen area, use several light effleurages, draining away from the periphery of the trauma and always moving toward the heart.

Repeat the kneading technique, progressing in a spiral fashion toward the center of the problem area, shaving half to 1 inch at a time. Alternate with effleurages at the completion of each kneading circle around the swollen area.

During the first application of the swelling technique to a traumatized area in the acute phase (first 24 hours), leave the dead center (1 inch diameter or more if needed) of the swelling site, because it is important to let the natural healing process take its course.

After the first 24 hours, the clotting of the bruised fibers will have taken place and you will be safe to massage the entire area with this swelling technique.

When in the chronic stage, after 72 hours, it is recommended that you apply some gentle frictions over the entire area to loosen and breakdown adhesions to maintain maximum flexibility between the muscle fibers, fascia and skin. Always monitor the feedback of your dog especially when doing such work. When there is a considerable decrease in the swelling, use more effleurage, progressively adding a little more pressure but never in a heavy manner. You may slightly increase the rhythm of your moves. Estimate the degree of inflammation and tenderness and adjust your pressure and pace accordingly.

At the end of your massage, apply cold hydrotherapy again to reduce nerve irritation and encourage vasoconstriction to further assist the drainage process. The cold application's secondary effect will contribute to even out the overall circulation of fluids in that particular area.

DURATION OF APPLICATION

The time frames given here apply only for the massage part of the swelling technique, not the hydrotherapy application.

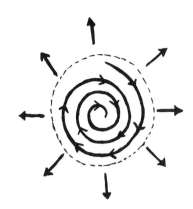

8.2   Schematic Diagram of Swelling Technique

Over a small area of 2 or 3 inches in diameter, the massage should not last more than 5 minutes in order to avoid irritation of the dermatomes (skin sensory nerve endings). Over a larger area, 10 to 15 inches in diameter, the application should last no more than 10 minutes. If the swollen area is very large a whole leg or hindquarter, do not exceed 15 minutes. Use palmar kneading instead of thumb kneading to cover more surface area. Remember that the tissues are very tender and a gentle pressure is enough to mechanically re-route the excess fluid. Always keep a relaxed rhythm of 1 move per second.

LOWER LEG SWELLING

When dealing with the swelling of the lower leg, gently but thoroughly massage the upper leg to stir up the circulation and clear the way before pushing the excess fluid upward. Ice massage does wonders for lower leg edema. When dealing with the foreleg you can flex the elbow to bring the lower leg horizontal with one hand and work the tendon thoroughly with the other hand using mostly effleurage moves. Here your overall treatment should not exceed 20 to 25 minutes, including hydrotherapy.

Follow this swelling technique with a cold hydrotherapy application (see chapter 5) to reduce the nerve irritation and to encourage vasoconstriction to further the drainage process. The secondary lasting vasodilatation effect of the cold application will regulate the overall fluid circulation.

FREQUENCY OF USING THE SWELLING TECHNIQUE

The degree of inflammation present in the tissues will determine the frequency of using this specialized technique. Evaluate the condition by checking the degree of swelling, the temperature level of the inflammation and the level of tenderness present. It is best to do several small sessions in the course of a few days to achieve a steady rate of recovery. By attempting large, extensive sessions in a short period you risk aggravating the inflammation and delaying the healing process.

If the inflammation is very strong in a small area, apply the swelling technique only once or twice a day (10 to 12 hours apart); if on a large area, just once a day. You can, however, apply cold hydrotherapy several times a day (up to 10 times) for 10 minutes at a time. If the inflammation is moderate, the swelling technique can be repeated 2 or 3 times a day with a minimum of 6 hours between sessions.

When dealing with a larger area such as a leg, you may work this technique twice daily. As the swelling goes down and the tissues becomes less tender, you can use a little more pressure and more effleurages. Be gentle and very careful in the acute stage, becoming more invasive gradually as the swelling heals. Remember to use hydrotherapy before, after, and in between the sessions to accentuate the drainage process and reduce the inflammation of the nerve endings.

In the case of a flare-up of an old injury, the relief of the swelling might take twice as many sessions as in an acute injury due to the chronic, recurrent aspect of the inflammation. If tenderness is present in the tissue, the use of cold hydrotherapy may be more beneficial than heat. If the nerves do not appear to be irritated, use heat or vascular flush (see chapter 5). After the swelling is definitely gone, resume a regular massage practice.

TRIGGER POINT TECHNIQUE

The trigger point technique is used to release and drain trigger points. A trigger point forms primarily as the result of toxin buildup (mostly lactic acid). Because of the toxicity in the fibers, an irritation of the local motor nerve endings develops. The term "trigger point" originates in the fact that pressure applied to that particular point will send a pain referral to other body parts. This referred pain is mostly caused by the presence and association of nerve endings throughout the muscle groups.

A trigger point is usually found in the belly part of a muscle. Depending on your dog's level and type of activity, trigger points can form in several muscles anywhere in the body. This condition occurs mostly in response to muscle tension (overuse) or nervous stress; it is sometimes due to a lack of activity (sluggish circulation). The hypertonicity or hypotonicity of the muscle fibers causes a decrease in blood circulation as well as a decrease in oxygen, resulting in a buildup of toxins. The increase in toxins in one particular area will trigger a nerve ending irritation.

Muscular tension is mostly due to overwork or overplay and not enough stretching or rest. Excess fatigue, nervous stress, restlessness or boredom can trigger the same muscular tension.

When the referred pain is of weak intensity, it is termed a silent trigger point; whereas one that sends strong sensations and is very sensitive to the touch is referred to as an active trigger point. Frequently, trigger points are found within symptom referral areas. Occasionally, one trigger point will have more than one referral area; these are called spill-over areas.

Trigger points feel like small nodules but they occasionally can appear as larger nodules; in any size, they are usually very tender. Trigger points give easily under pressure and release fairly quickly. Hot hydrotherapy application over the specific area will contribute greatly to the effectiveness of your trigger point technique. It will loosen the tissue fibers and boost the circulation in the area. Use hot packs or hot towels (see chapter 5). Start with the

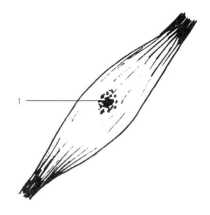

8.3   Schematic Diagram of a Trigger Point

(1) Toxin buildup in the belly of the muscle, resulting in a trigger point

SEW approach to warm up the muscles. Then use thumb kneadings to loosen the muscle fibers and locate the area of most congestion and tenderness.

When you find a trigger point, be gentle. Use a light pressure as you apply your thumb directly over the nodule. Hold the pressure until the muscle relaxes. The release process may take just a few seconds for recently formed trigger points, or up to 1 minute for more chronic trigger points. Follow the release with lots of effleurages to ensure proper drainage of this area.

Your initial touch of the trigger point will likely be very tender to your dog. Monitor your animal's feedback and keep reassuring him with a soft voice. After 10 to 20 seconds, the tenderness will decrease considerably.

When working with an acute trigger point, you should hold a light pressure,

2 to 5 pounds, for most of the application only raising the pressure slightly to a maximum of 10 pounds at the end when you feel the trigger point releasing.

When working with a silent trigger point, you may consider progressively raising your pressure to 15 pounds depending on the muscular mass you are working on and the dog's reaction. When treating a trigger point in the brachiocephalicus muscle of the neck, for example, you might consider squeezing or pinching the trigger point between your thumb and index finger. Use the same pressure and duration as you would in any other situation.

Do not use more pressure than necessary; trigger points can be overtreated. The ideal pressure is the one that gives a sensation somewhere between pleasure and pain. Evaluate the pressure applied relative to your dog's feedback; watch his eyes. You may apply a continuous pressure or consider alternating pressures (for example, light to heavier, back to light, 2 or 3 times). If the pressure is too heavy, the dog will certainly let you know. Play it safe!

Once released, trigger point areas should be drained thoroughly with plenty of effleurages. Then, to further the treatment, use light frictions along the length of the whole muscle fiber—or the whole muscle bundle—in which the trigger point was located. This, along with the effleurage, will increase the drainage. Drainage after trigger point release is most important. As you break down a long-standing buildup of toxins, you must move those toxins into the circulation to

avoid creating a worse condition. Drainage will also bring fresh blood, new oxygen and nutrients to greatly assist the healing process. Use the WES approach.

The area where the trigger point(s) was located may be very sore for a few hours, or even a day or so, due to the inflammation of the nerve endings. In that case, wait a day or two before working deeply on the same area again. In the meantime, apply light effleurages and wringings plus gentle finger frictions daily if possible to increase the blood circulation through that area and to assist recovery. If some degree of inflammation is present, use cold hydrotherapy after the treatment to soothe the nerve endings and boost the circulation.

The trigger point technique is used very often as part of the maintenance routine (see chapter 9) and in sport massage treatments after heavy exercise or play. We recommend that you lightly exercise your dog immediately after this type of work if he is not fatigued. Gentle exercise such as walking will allow the muscles to recover their full contractile power and elasticity, flush fresh blood through the fibers and maximize the effect of the treatment.

STRESS POINT TECHNIQUE

The stress point technique is used to release stress points. Stress points are microspasms involving only a few fibers out of a whole bundle of fibers. However, these microspasm stress points can turn into full-blown muscle spasms.

If a stress point is not inflamed, it is referred to as a dormant stress point. If a stress point is inflamed, it is referred to as an active stress point, which will display more tenderness and will eventually produce heat and swelling. Many dogs experience tight muscles resulting in reduced muscle action (shorter stride or lameness) due to stress point development within these muscles.

HOW STRESS POINTS FORM

Stress points form as a result of great mechanical stress, which causes micro-tearing of the muscle fibers. Heavy training, repetitive actions, weight overload, strenuous effort and so on are all examples of great mechanical stress.

Stress points also develop as a response to trauma such as a bump, a fall or as a result of overstretching. After an injury and during the recovery stage, the muscular compensation developing in the rest of a dog's body will trigger formation of other stress points within the compensatory muscles. For example, a dog with a sore wrist will develop compensatory stress points in the shoulder muscles as well as in the muscle attaching the scapula to the rest of the body. If really lame, the dog will switch his weight onto the other legs to relieve pressure on the sore wrist causing a great deal of muscular strain on the other limbs and resulting in new stress point formation.

It is important to remember that the inflammation process—the body's natural healing response to any trauma—can lead to a vicious circle of pain, tension,

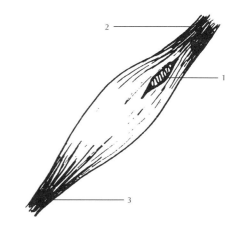

8.4 *Schematic Diagram of a Stress Point*

> *(1) stress point, usually found by the origin tendon*
> *(2) origin tendon*
> *(3) insertion tendon*

inflammation, more pain and so on. The inflammation process could result in the formation of more stress points. A bad case of a sore back/hip is a good example of this phenomenon. Keep the inflammation under control by using hydrotherapy (see chapter 5) to cool the area and maintain the inflammation at a healthy level. Use lots of effleurages to ensure proper flow of blood to the area bringing fresh oxygen and nutrients.

WHERE STRESS POINTS FORM

Stress points can be found anywhere in the muscular structure of the dog. Due to the nature of the dog's locomotor system, there are some well-known areas of the skeleton and related specific muscle groups where stress points are usually found.

Stress points will most often develop at a muscle's origin tendon. The origin tendon is the tendon that anchors the muscle to the stable, non-movable body part during a concentric contraction. The origin tendon tends to be quite strong and of good size because it is the anchor attachment for the muscle and therefore sustains great mechanical strain. The other tendon, the insertion tendon, attaches the muscle to the movable part. This tendon is not as strong or as large as the origin tendon, but sometimes it will show stress, especially during isometric contractions to stabilize the body and eccentric contractions when absorbing great tension (during landing, for example).

The dog, like a human, works all of his body at once. Muscle tightening does not remain in an isolated area. It transmits from one muscle to another, from one muscle group to another. As one group tightens up, the antagonist group must compensate for the loss of movement and therefore experiences extra stress. You will find several stress points during a treatment. Some are related; some are not.

How Stress Points Feel

A stress point feels like a spot of hardened, rigid tissue about the size of the end of your little finger or less. It does not move under the fingers, might be slightly swollen and will feel tender to the dog when touched. Also a tight line of muscle fibers within the muscle bundle associated with the stress point will be felt across the muscle.

During an acute stage or an inflammation flair-up, stress points will show up very quickly. They are easily detectable because of their tenderness and the presence of heat and swelling. If the stress point area appears inflamed, use cold hydrotherapy (see chapter 5) to numb the nerve endings prior to your treatment. Apply the swelling technique if necessary and follow with the stress point technique. When inflammation is present, work very lightly, progressing gently into deeper massage over a few sessions to relieve the inflammation.

During chronic stages, the stress points will be more difficult to detect because the symptoms of heat and swelling are less evident. But with practice, you will develop a feel for stress points and will recognize them easily. If no inflammation is present, you might consider using heat or vascular flush over the area to loosen the fibers prior to your treatment.

When Stress Points Form

Stress points can form at any time, especially when the dog is under a lot of strain, is fatigued by intense playing/training, has been hurt by trauma (blow, fall), has chronic pain from an old injury or has a chronic condition such as arthritis or rheumatism. Older dogs show arthritic deterioration in leg joints where the consequent pain causes muscle tension. This muscle tension triggers more arthritic degeneration in the joints.

Massage can help break this cycle of muscle tension and stress point buildup.

How Dogs Respond to Stress Point Work

The animal's response to your work will vary greatly with the degree of inflammation present in the muscle tissue. With stress points, the pain reaction you get in relation to your pressure indicates the severity of the stress. To assess the stress point, start with a light pressure, which you then progressively build up.

From experience in human therapy practice, pain caused by a stress point is not normally as sharp as that in a trigger point, but it can be severe on occasion and especially during acute inflammation. The initial contact on the stress point may elicit some tenderness, but soon a feeling of relief will replace the original discomfort.

When a stress point is dormant (nonactive), mild pressure (8 to 12 pounds) applied to it will cause a skin twitching reaction. After a few minutes, a general release of the muscle worked on will occur. When a stress point is active (inflamed), the reaction will be more pronounced. As you apply light pressure (3 to 5 pounds) to an active stress point, you will notice excessive skin twitching and flinching; the animal will pull away from the pressure. If the reaction is sharp or if the adjacent muscles are showing excessive tightness, you might suspect that the muscle is close to full spasm. Be very gentle and methodical in your approach.

Stress Point Technique Outline

The stress point technique consists of two stages. One deals with the Golgi apparatus nerve cell, the other deals with the muscle spindle nerve cell. As you locate a stress point, identify the muscle it belongs to.

The Golgi

A thorough massage of the origin tendon with pressure applied toward the bone will stretch the sensory nerve endings—Golgi nerve cell—located in the tendons. While being stretched, the Golgi nerve cell will send nerve impulses to the brain and cause a reflex through the nervous system. The reflex will relax the corresponding motor nerve, which is responsible for this stress point. The nervous reflex may take from a few seconds to a few minutes to occur. Small stress points may release very quickly, while more chronic stress points may take several minutes. Do not overwork them.

If the stress point area appears inflamed, use cold hydrotherapy to numb the nerve endings. Otherwise, if the area does not appear inflamed, consider using heat or vascular flush over the area to loosen the fibers (see chapter 5).

Start your technique with the SEW approach to warm up the area. Proceed with a thorough kneading massage over the origin tendon where you have located the stress point. With your thumb or fingertips apply a gentle pressure (2 or 3 pounds) on the stress point to establish the initial contact and evaluate the degree of inflammation. Apply your pressure on the stress point and toward the bone where the muscle anchors. Progressively increase your pressure to 5 pounds, and then up to 10 to 15 pounds as the stress point release occurs.

Observe your animal's reaction as you proceed and adjust accordingly. Hold the pressure until you feel the stress point let go. Follow with lots of effleurages to thoroughly drain the area. If after a minute no release has happened, progressively release your pressure, intersperse with a few effleurages, and repeat the procedure of applying pressure to the stress point for another minute or until it releases.

THE MUSCLE SPINDLE

The second stage of this technique consists of working the muscle spindle nerve cell. Use the one-hand or double-hand friction move back and forth two or three times across the length of the muscle bundle to gently work the muscle spindle nerve ending. Move your fingertips very gently and perpendicularly to the grain of the muscle fibers all along their course. Using a medium pressure of 8 to 12 pounds, intersperse your gentle frictions with effleurages every 20 seconds to drain the area. This will reset nerve awareness and will fully relax the muscle. Also, this gentle frictioning will loosen the tight fibers, increase circulation through the muscle, restore free motion to the fibers and decrease painful symptoms.

Be aware that if you friction the muscle spindle too vigorously or with too much pressure (15 to 20 pounds), it will stretch the muscle spindle and will cause the muscle to react by contracting. Be gentle during this phase of the technique.

Follow up with the WES approach to bring in new blood, nutrients and oxygen to the site. The muscle will feel better immediately. The dog should be lightly exercised (walk/trot) immediately after the treatment. When the dog is warm, use stretching exercises (see chapter 4) to further the release of the affected muscle groups.

The stress point technique is very efficient when properly applied. If underworked, a stress point will still present the same symptoms with very little or no improvement. If you do not feel any improvement after working on a stress point for 2 or 3 minutes, stop. Overworking the tissues will aggravate the inflammation (heat, swelling, pain), especially in chronic tension cases. Sometimes it takes several treatments to relieve a stress point.

If inflammation is present, use the ice cup technique (see chapter 5 for more about hydrotherapy) after your treatment to cool the nerve endings and elicit vasodilation. Give the dog a couple of days of rest before further massage in that area. Keep records of your work and of the results produced (see chapter 13). Regular practice will allow you to experiment and gain expertise.

THE ORIGIN-INSERTION TECHNIQUE

The origin-insertion technique will release muscle hypertonicity (contracture) and full muscle spasm, as well as strengthen muscle weakness (hypotonicity). The origin-insertion technique is simply the stress point technique applied to both the origin and the insertion tendons of a muscle.

Origin-insertion refers to the origin and the insertion tendons of a muscle. The origin tendon is the muscle part that anchors to the most stable, least movable bone. The insertion tendon attaches the muscle to the movable part, so that during contraction the insertion is brought closer to the origin. The origin tendon is usually stronger and bigger than the insertion tendon because its anchor attachment sustains greater stress. This stress is responsible for most of the problems found close to the origin tendons.

Contracture can be found anywhere in the belly of the muscle. Contracture is a hypertonic state in which muscle fibers cannot release their contractile power. Many motor nerve impulses resulting from high stress, pain and inflammation cause the muscle fibers to contract indefinitely. Contractures are responsible for the decrease of muscle action that results in congestion, a lack of fluid circulation in the muscle fibers, as well as restricted movement (for example, a shorter stride).

By thoroughly massaging the origin and the insertion tendons (Golgi sensory nerve endings) and the whole muscle bundle (muscle spindle nerve endings), the origin-insertion technique will send relaxation impulses to the brain. In response, the corresponding motor nerve signal causing the muscle to remain contracted will cease, releasing the spasm. This release might occur quickly or not depending on the stress level, the severity of the spasm, and whether the spasm is associated with a trauma or with a wound. Sometimes a spasm will not release until several hours after the treatment.

To derive the maximum benefit from this technique, you need a thorough knowledge of the muscle group on

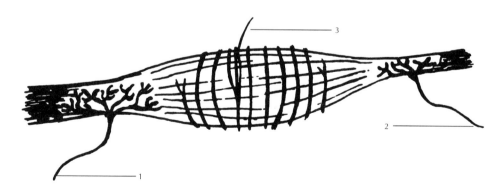

8.5   The Origin-Insertion Technique

(1) Golgi sensory nerve cell by the origin tendon
(2) Golgi sensory nerve cell by the insertion tendon
(3) muscle spindle sensory nerve cell by the muscle bundle

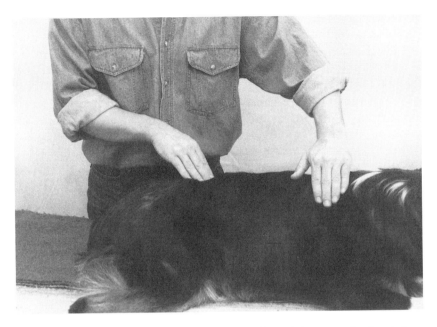

8.6   The Origin-Insertion Technique: Performed here on the longissimus dorsi muscle.

which you are working. Knowing where the muscles attach and their direction is most important to the effectiveness of the treatment.

When dealing with a full spasm, remember that your dog is feeling a lot of pain from this condition. Use cold hydrotherapy (see chapter 5) to numb the pain and lots of strokings to comfort your animal before you start applying the origin-insertion technique.

THE ORIGIN-INSERTION TECHNIQUE OUTLINE

After you locate the problem and ascertain which muscle you need to work on, begin with the SEW approach to gently warm up the muscle tissues. Then use a gentle but firm double-thumb kneading over the origin tendon, pressing it against the bone away from the belly of the muscle. Apply pressure at approximately 5 to 10 pounds (up to 15 to 20 on large muscle groups) for approximately 2 minutes. Intersperse with some effleurages every 20 to 30 seconds.

When finished on the origin tendon, thoroughly drain the area you worked on with several effleurages. Then repeat the kneading and effleurage procedure in the same fashion on the insertion tendon.

When finished, drain the entire muscle area with thorough effleurages. Next, using your fingertips, gently friction the whole muscle across the fibers back and forth 2 or 3 times along the entire muscle length. Finish with the WES approach to ensure a thorough drainage.

Depending on the spasm's severity and the degree of inflammation present in the tissue, the origin-insertion technique should not continue for more than 10 minutes. Avoid overworking the area because this will only aggravate the situation. It is better to repeat the application several times over a few days rather than risk irritating the nerve endings or worsening the inflammation in the muscle fibers during the first session.

In most acute stages, the contracture or spasm will release shortly—within 30 minutes or a few of hours—after the first application.

If the contracture is in a chronic stage, it may take several sessions to produce a positive result.

In the case of a torn muscle, the origin-insertion technique is contraindicated in the acute stage (first 24 hours) and only applied in a very gentle way in the sub-acute phase.

When using this origin-insertion technique to strengthen a weak muscle, you need to reverse the direction of your kneading pressure by pressing toward the belly of the muscle instead of toward the bone. This manual stretching of the Golgi nerve will result in a tonifying reaction onto the muscle. When working a weak muscle, you only need to apply this technique for about 5 to 10 minutes at a time proportional to the muscle size. Repeating the treatment several times over a few days will show tremendous improvements.

In all cases, follow with the appropriate stretch (see chapter 4), but only if there are no torn muscle fibers!

Cold hydrotherapy (see chapter 5) is beneficial before and after treatment. Cold hydrotherapy reduces nerve irritability and cools down the inflammation. The vasoconstriction followed by the vasodilation reaction will flush the muscle and provide more blood with new nutrients and oxygen. Heat would be more appropriate when dealing with a weak muscle.

The origin-insertion technique is used regularly in maintenance and preventive massages to stimulate and strengthen both over-exercised muscles and weak muscles.

The various techniques presented here will sharpen your skills. They will ensure the best results in maintaining your dog's fitness or assisting in his recovery.

9

A massage routine is a series of massage moves or techniques arranged in a specific order to achieve the best results in the shortest time. A few examples are the relaxation, maintenance and recuperation routines that were created to address particular situations in the most effective way possible. These routines will contribute to the maintenance and preventive care of your animal while simultaneously giving you feedback on his general health and training level.

When a dog is restless, scared, or after a long journey, a relaxation routine will ease him fairly quickly. For the exercising dog, the maintenance routine will keep the muscular structure free from trigger and stress points, improve your dog's performance and make him feel good. When your dog has been training heavily, the recuperation routine will help shorten the recovery time and prevent the tightening up and stiffening of the locomotor structures. The warm up and cool down routines will assist the animal just before and after exercising. The trouble spot routine

will help prevent muscular problems in the heavily exercised dog.

To ensure proper maintenance, most routines should be applied on a regular basis. Such a schedule will give you frequent feedback on the physical and emotional condition of your animal while contributing to the preventive aspect of your training program. Applying these routines regularly will not only develop your dog's confidence during your work, but will also encourage the animal to become deeply relaxed and trusting, responding fully to your massages.

The relaxation routine can be applied at any time. It is mainly used to make initial contact with the animal, before and after traveling, when putting him to rest, before a show, after a fright and so on. When done in a shorter version, the relaxation routine can be used to start any form of massage.

If the dog is in an average training program, the maintenance routines should be done regularly once or twice a week. If the dog is participating in a competitive more demanding program, maintenance routines should be used on a daily basis.

The recuperation routine should be given after every heavy training session. When a heavy training program ends, apply this routine daily for a few days until the transition to a slower pace program is complete.

Massage routines should be considered regular practice for the good health of your animal. To ensure the effectiveness of these routines, it is best to work on the dog in a quiet location, free from distractions and noise.

With practice you will become familiar with the routines outlined in this chapter. The types of movement, the rhythm and the pressure are particular to each routine; they are selected and placed in specific sequences to ensure specific results. Always start working with a gentle approach, progressively increasing your pressure and rhythm when needed.

You will be able to add your own touches and eventually create your own routines according to your goals and the conditions you are treating. Trust your own judgment and be creative. At the beginning, for safety and effectiveness, follow the guidelines given here. These routines are designed for healthy animals. If abnormal problems arise or there is strong indication of an inflammation, check with a veterinarian or registered massage therapist before proceeding.

THE RELAXATION MASSAGE ROUTINE

Dogs, like humans, experience stress of different kinds ranging from the physical (exercises, training schedules, workload) to the emotional (abuse, boredom, lack of love or kindness, anxiety, fear). When a dog is stressed, his body will show tension, but the original stress itself is in the brain. The purpose of the relaxation routine is to relax the animal and relieve stress in a quick and efficient way.. The relaxation routine concentrates on the nervous system only, using mostly pure nervous reflex massage moves over the spinal column (the neck, the back, the sacrum and the tail) to elicit a parasympathetic nervous response (see chapter 2 for more about the nervous system).

The relaxation routine requires very little pressure (a maximum of 2 or 3 pounds) and the rhythm of your movements should be very smooth (1 move per second on average). This routine will achieve positive results over the course of the first few treatments. The relaxation achieved will clear nervous tension and blockages while regenerating the flow of vital energy through the spine to the rest of the body.

The relaxation routine is highly effective in inducing deep relaxation at once and is good to use when approaching a dog for its first massage. It will induce great relaxation and a strong relief of nervous stress—it might even put your dog to sleep. Your dog will feel an overall improvement as a result of these treatments. Even dogs of strong character will

9.1 Relaxation Massage Routine Outline

soften drastically after several relaxing massage sessions, becoming more enjoyable companions.

THE RELAXATION MASSAGE ROUTINE OUTLINE

Use this routine when starting any other routine or massage treatment. The relaxation massage routine also can be applied before and after traveling, before, during and after competition, in the event of a scare, and if the dog has become restless from boredom. When giving an animal his first massage, employ this routine, including the head massage routine, to give it a complete feeling of relaxation.

Before beginning the routine, it is important to stand beside the dog for a few minutes to connect with him. Spend a few moments gently stroking the dog's neck and the base of the ears.

1. POLL WORK

Start with 3 clockwise and then 12 counterclockwise gentle, small circular movements with the fingertips, just behind the ears to connect with the animal for a few seconds. To reinforce the relaxed atmosphere, talk quietly to him. With your right hand, massage the crest of the neck with light muscle squeezing, 2 or 3 pounds pressure at the most, starting directly behind the pole and over a few inches. Apply 20 to 30 gentle muscle squeezings to trigger the parasympathetic nervous response that allows relaxation. The dog will probably lower his head as a response to your work.

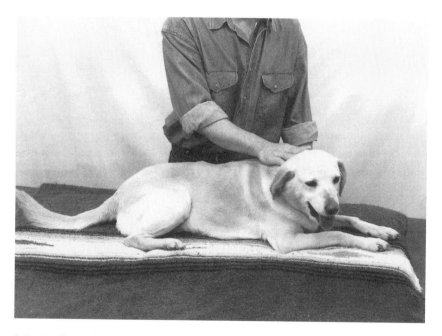

9.2   Poll Work: *Relaxation Routine*

2. EAR WORK

Gently pull the ears from the base to the tips stretching them backward. Gently and very lightly rub the tips between your fingers for a few seconds. This will soothe the dog. If your dog does not like his ears being worked, skip this part and spend more time massaging the crest of the neck behind the pole.

3. NECK WORK

With both hands, use the muscle squeezing move along the whole upper area of the neck from the base of the skull down to the shoulders in one pass. Your pressure should be firm but no heavier than 5 to 8 pounds, and your rhythm smooth and slow with 1 muscle squeeze per 2 seconds. This particular approach will have a very

soothing effect on the animal. Most dogs lower their heads willingly in this sequence and you might want to repeat with a second pass to reinforce this feeling of relaxation.

4. NECK ROCKING

This is for large dogs with very tense or thickly muscled necks; smaller animals would probably not enjoy this movement. In a very gentle manner, use some stroking moves in the direction of the hair over the entire neck. Then employ some very gentle neck rocking movements to further relax the whole neck. To do so, place one hand on the upper area of the neck and your other hand on the windpipe for support, then gently rock the top of the neck back and forth. Build

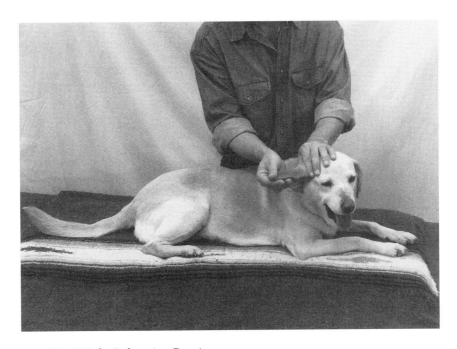

9.3 **Ear Work:** *Relaxation Routine*

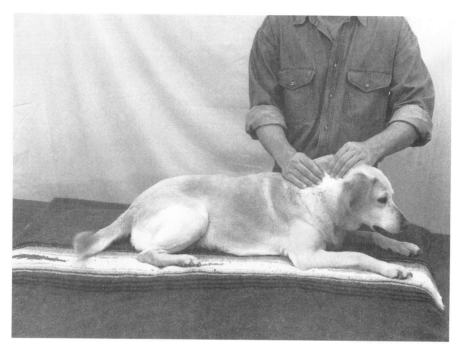

9.4   Neck–Crest Work: Relaxation Routine

up slowly to a rhythm of 1 movement per second. Start at the upper neck and slowly, over 6 to 8 rocking motions, go down to the shoulders. This will greatly loosen the large muscle group of the neck.

5. UPPER SHOULDER WORK

After the neck rocking, stroke the neck downward and start to massage the whole upper shoulder area (both sides) with very smooth muscle squeezing. Be gentle throughout. Use 3 to 5 pounds pressure for approximately 1 minute. Intersperse with light strokings every 30 seconds for 3 to 5 seconds at a time.

6. BACK WORK

Follow with 2 or 3 light long strokes over the entire back. Keep the pressure very light at 1 or 2 pounds maximum and the rhythm very smooth.

7. SACRUM WORK

As you finish your back work, place your right hand over the sacrum bone. Hold it there with a light vibration for 10 to 30 seconds. Then make 3 slow clockwise circular motions, reversing to counterclockwise motions for 15 to 20 circles. This particular move will strongly stimulate the parasympathetic nervous response (chapter 2).

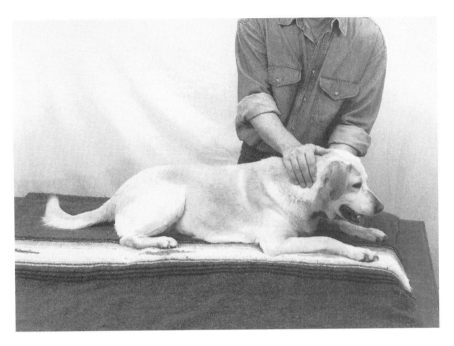

9.5   Neck Rocking Movement: *Relaxation Routine*

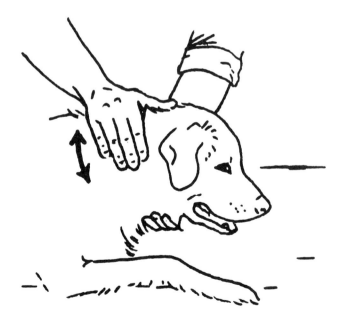

9.6   Neck Rocking Movement: *Relaxation Routine*

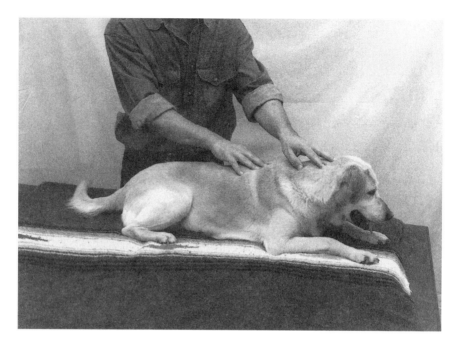

9.7   Upper Shoulder Work: *Relaxation Routine*

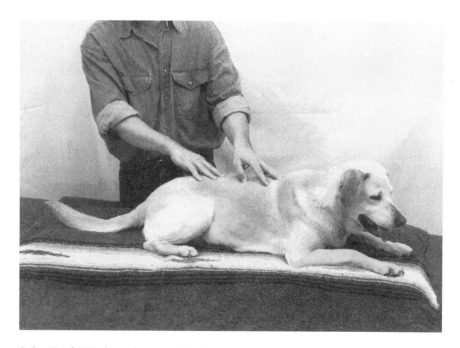

9.8   Back Work: *Relaxation Routine*

8. TAIL WORK

After the sacrum work, switch the position of your right hand with your left hand to keep contact with the dog. With the right hand, use gentle point pressure along the tail bone, then the rump and flow to the next move. Pick up the tail with your right hand; take the tail a few inches from its base, bringing it upward. Use your left hand as well to stretch the tail into a question mark (see Figure 9.11).

Gently move the tail in a circle, 3 times clockwise and 3 times counterclockwise. Take note of any movement restriction on either side of the tail; this is a sign of muscle tension in the tail muscles and the hindquarters.

At this point, move yourself to the rear of the dog and pull on his tail very gently. Hold this stretch for approximately 30 seconds to a minute unless the dog shows signs of discomfort. Usually the dog responds positively by pulling against your traction. Stretching the tail will contribute to and increase the dog's relaxation tremendously.

While stretching the tail with one hand, use the thumb and fingers of the other hand to gently work each vertebra from the base of the tail downward with a few muscle squeezings. Reverse the hands if you prefer.

Take note of the tail's flexibility, any tender spots or points of possible inflammation. Release the tail stretch progressively and

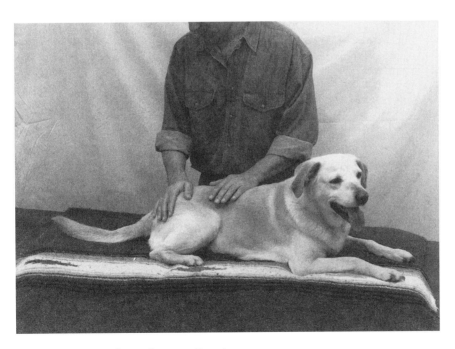

9.9 Sacrum Work: *Relaxation Routine*

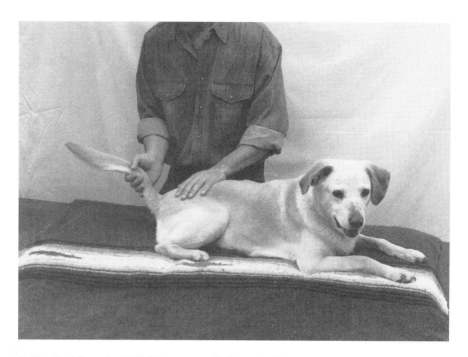

9.10   Raising the Tail Movement: *Relaxation Routine*

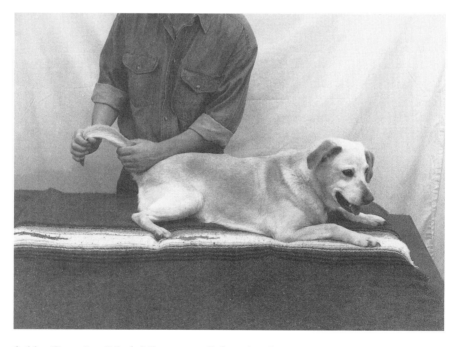

9.11   Question Mark Movement: *Relaxation Routine*

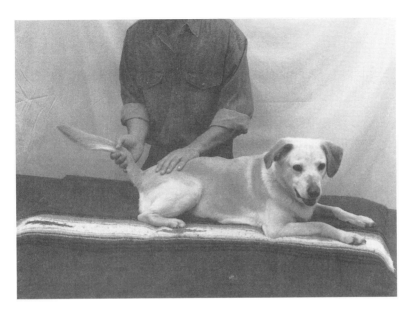

9.12   Turning Tail Movement: *Relaxation Routine*

9.13   Stretching the Tail Out: *Carefully and gently work each vertebra with soft muscle squeezing moves, relaxation routine.*

then stroke the hindquarters and sacrum area for a few seconds.

Warning! When you start stretching the tail and it feels "loose" at its attachment site (with half an inch give before the actual stretch starts), stop at once. You could be hurting the dog. The looseness means that the dog has a fairly common joint problem at the tail junction; as you start pulling the tail, you could produce a strain. If the dog shows discomfort, inflammation or other abnormal symptoms on palpation of this area, skip the stretching and check with your veterinarian.

9. LEG WORK

After the tail work, proceed with a gentle stroking down the legs. Never lose hand contact with the dog. Use 2 to 3 strokings on the way down the leg and 2 or 3 on the way up, adding a few more over the upper body as you move from leg to leg. Since you are already at the rear, start with the hind legs (as shown in photo 9.14). Then, with a few stroking movements, move to the front legs, and repeat the same approach on the front legs.

Pick up each leg in a gentle manner. When the leg is flexed, move it gently in a small circle inward, then forward, to the outside, then back. Start again, repeating the movement 2 or 3 times. This action will further the relaxation and the feeling of release in the legs and indirectly over the rest of the body. Be gentle! This relaxation routine should take from 10 to 15 minutes depending on the dog's size. You can take longer if you want, but the point of this routine is to initiate the relaxation reflex in a short time frame. Approximately 10 minutes is ideal.

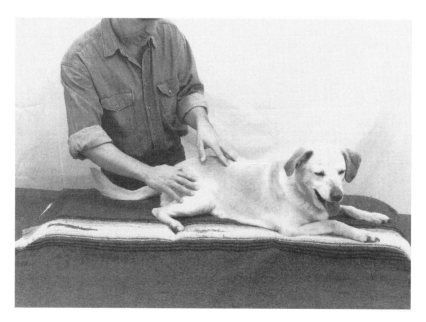

9.14 *Stroking the Hind Legs Down:* *Relaxation Routine*

SHORT VERSION OF THE RELAXATION MASSAGE ROUTINE

When you use the relaxation routine as a starter before another routine, a shorter version of the relaxation routine can be used. Skip the muscle squeezings over the crest of the neck, the neck rocking, the upper shoulder work, and the leg work at the end. Perform the routine movements in the following order:

1. Start with circular movements right behind the upper neck.

2. Use strokings down the neck, over the back and all the way to the sacrum.

3. Work the sacrum.

4. Work the tail. When finished with the tail, flow back to the neck using strokings and go on to the other routine or technique.

In the early stage of connecting with the dog, it is highly recommended that you use the full relaxation routine until the animal gets used to the relaxation associated with this particular work. Experience shows that this routine outline works very well. It won't take long before the dog associates his relaxation with your work. So with practice, you will be surprised how quickly your dog will feel relaxed.

THE MAINTENANCE MASSAGE ROUTINE

This routine is intended to keep the muscular and skeletal structure fit, to assist circulation of body fluids and to remove toxins. The maintenance massage routine also gives you a chance to evaluate and massage all muscle conditions (tension, knots, stress points and trigger points) and to detect any other abnormal symptoms. At any time in the maintenance routine, you can add appropriate techniques (see chapter 8) to deal with particular situations such as swellings, stress points or trigger points. If any abnormal problems should arise, please check with your veterinarian before proceeding with your massage.

Remember that on your first contact with the animal your pressure should be light, becoming firmer as you progress into the massage.

MAINTENANCE MASSAGE ROUTINE OUTLINE

Connect with the animal for a few seconds by talking quietly and gently massaging the upper neck with light muscle squeezings.

1. Start at the base of the neck with the SEW approach (chapter 8) covering the entire neck. Then use muscle squeezings along the top of the neck from the ears all the way to the shoulders. With thumb or finger kneadings, thoroughly work the various neck muscles. Intersperse with effleurages every 10 seconds. Your pressure should be light at the beginning, 2 or 3 pounds, progressing to a firmer touch of 8 to 10 pounds pressure. Your overall rhythm should be smooth—1 to 2 movements per

9.15   *Relaxation Massage Routine Short Version Outline*

9.16 *Maintenance Massage Routine Outline*

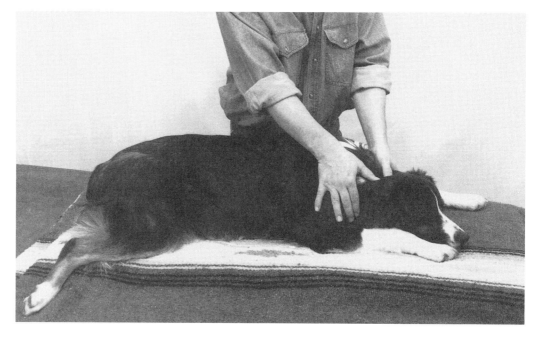

9.17   Upper Neck Work: *With double thumb kneading, maintenance routine*

9.18   Neck Work: *With double thumb kneading, maintenance routine*

second. Consider using gentle hand frictions to loosen the muscles. Finish by draining the neck with the WES approach (chapter 8).

2. Moving to the withers area, start with the SEW approach, then use muscle squeezings, thumb kneadings and gentle frictions to work thoroughly all of the muscle attachments. Intersperse every 10 seconds with effleurages (5 to 8 pound pressure) and finish with the WES approach before moving to the shoulder.

3. Use the SEW approach to warm up the entire shoulder area. Then use light kneadings (thumbs, fingers or palms) and gentle finger frictions, interspersed with effleurages, along the muscle of the scapula.

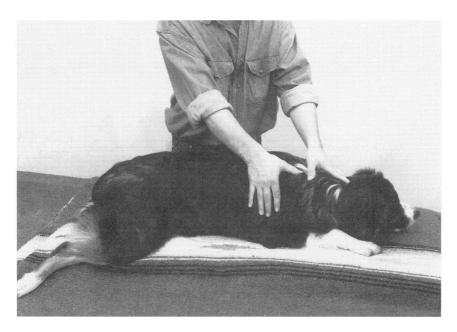

9.19 Withers Work: *With double thumb kneading, interspersed with effleurage, maintenance routine*

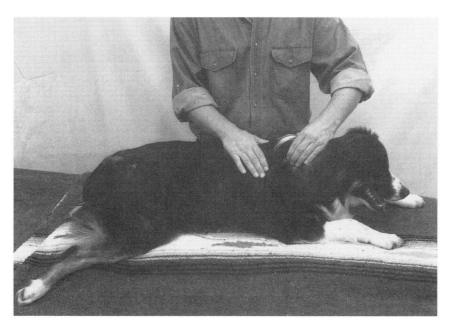

9.20 Lower Neck and Withers Work: *With muscle squeezings, maintenance routine*

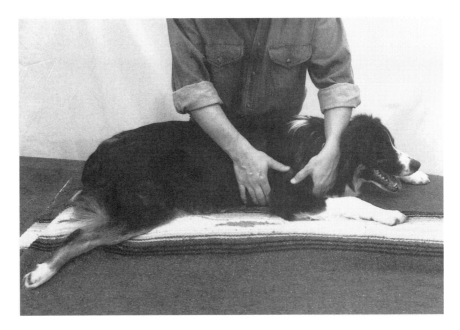

9.21 Shoulder Work: *With deep double thumb kneading, interspersed with effleurage, maintenance routine*

The serratus thoracis muscle often shows tension; use compression moves to loosen the fibers of this muscle, followed by gentle finger frictions. Drain the area thoroughly with the WES approach.

4. To work the leg, begin by gently stroking down the foreleg for a grounding effect. Then, progress with the SEW approach. Starting at the point of shoulder, use muscle squeezings, picking-ups, kneadings and gentle frictions, interspersed with effleurages, over the triceps muscle as well as the fleshy part of the flexor and extensor muscle groups. Gentle muscle squeezings, gentle frictions and thumb kneadings will loosen the tendons and stimulate the blood circulation all the way down to the paw; intersperse with effleurages going up the entire leg. Finish the leg with the WES approach.

5. Gently weave your strokings over to the front chest and complete the SEW approach over that area. Then use large kneadings, muscle squeezings, vibrations, shakings, gentle kneadings and compressions to massage the pectoral muscles and the point of the shoulder. Intersperse with effleurages every 20 to 30 seconds. Be creative. Then use the WES approach over the area and weave your strokings back over the shoulder all the way to the withers.

6. Use the SEW approach over the back and up and down the spine to stir up the circulation. Follow with light tapotements on the back

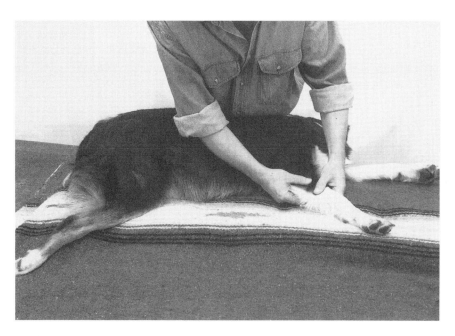

9.22 Foreleg Work: *With deep double thumb kneading, interspersed with effleurage, maintenance routine*

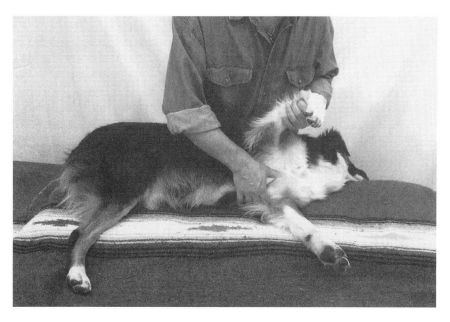

9.23 Chest Work: *With deep double thumb kneading, interspersed with effleurage, maintenance routine*

9.24   Back Work: *With tapotements, interspersed with effleurage, maintenance routine*

muscles to reach deep into the muscle structures along the spine. Intersperse with effleurages every 30 seconds on average. Finger or palmar kneadings and light frictions will help loosen the fibers of the longissimus muscle group of the back. Finish the back with the WES approach.

Use large wringings interspersed with effleurages up and down the thorax (ribcage) 2 or 3 times. Use light kneadings between the ribs and intersperse with effleurages toward the heart. You can use large shakings to stimulate the circulation over the chest area. Do not overdo the shakings as this may be more stressful than enjoyable to the animal. You may consider using tapotement moves in the form of light (3 to 5 pounds of pressure) clapping/cupping and hacking to deeply stimulate the circulation. Always follow with thorough effleurages. Also consider using the skin rolling move as it is very efficient in keeping the skin and underlying fascia loose.

7. Moving to the gluteus and hamstring muscles, use the SEW approach to warm up the area. Apply tapotements and compressions to stir up the circulation and to loosen the fibers of this large muscle group. Use thumbs, fingers or palmar kneadings and gentle finger frictions along the length of the fibers of all the muscle groups of the hindquarters. Intersperse with effleurages toward the stifle and finish this area with the WES approach.

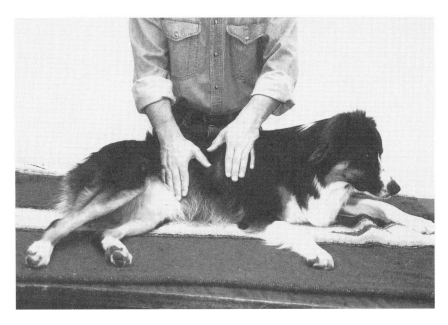

9.25   Ribcage Work: *With thumb kneading, interspersed with effleurage, maintenance routine*

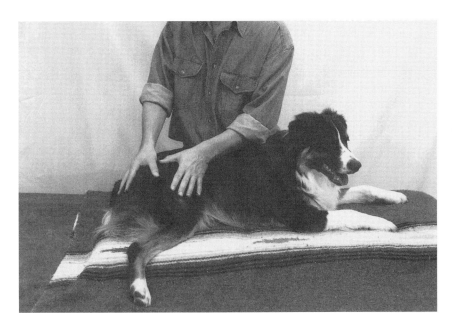

9.26   Gluteus Work: *With deep double thumb kneading, interspersed with effleurage, maintenance routine*

9.27   Hamstrings Work: *With muscle squeezing, interspersed with effleurage, maintenance routine*

8. Begin with the SEW approach on the hind legs, then effleurage upward toward the flank area. Use gentle muscle squeezings, kneadings and gentle frictions, all interspersed with effleurages every 10 seconds over the fleshy part of the flexor and extensor muscle group of the hind leg. Drain thoroughly upward starting from the top of the leg and working your way down. Once at the bottom of the leg, effleurage from the paw to the stifle in one long stroke; repeat to cover all aspects of the limb. Gentle muscle squeezings, gentle frictions and thumb kneadings will loosen the tendons and stimulate the blood circulation to the muscle all the way down to the paw; finish the hind leg with the WES approach going up the entire leg.

9. With effleurages, flow back to the thorax area (trunk).

Gently reposition your dog and repeat this sequence on the other side of his body. The overall routine can last between 20 and 30 minutes depending on your goal, the temperament of the dog and his size. Keep it on the short side when in the early stage of massaging your dog. With repetition, your dog will become more receptive to your massage work. After he has become accustomed to your work, it will not be unusual for a maintenance massage routine to last an hour and a half for a large dog.

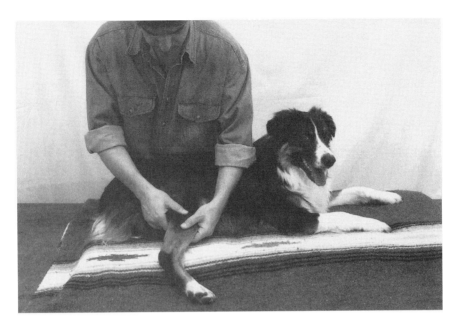

9.28 **Hind Legs Work:** *With thumb kneading, interspersed with effleurage, maintenance routine*

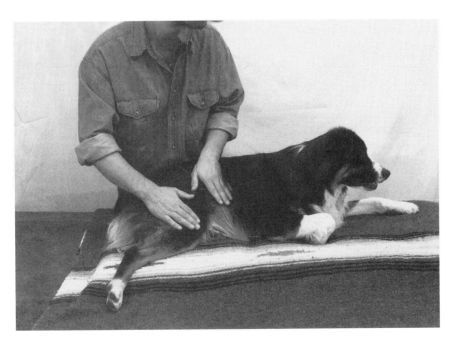

9.29 **Hind Leg Drainage Work:** *With effleurage, maintenance routine*

9.30   Thorax Drainage Work: *With effleurage, maintenance routine*

The maintenance massage routine will give you feedback on the physiological state of your dog and will help you detect problems early and prevent any small problems from becoming more serious. As you find trigger points, stress points, swellings and inflammations, take notes and apply the appropriate techniques (chapter 8). Always follow with lots of effleurages.

The maintenance routine also is a wonderful tool for maintaining and increasing the dog's performance. Regular use of the routine, at least once a week, will give you feedback on the quality of your training and warn you of any potential overworked muscles and tendons. For highly trained dogs, this routine should be applied at least every second day.

Due to the frequency of the massage application, you will find that 20 to 30 minute sessions are sufficient to keep your dog in top shape and will prevent any serious muscular problems from hampering your dog's performance.

THE RECUPERATION MASSAGE ROUTINE

The recuperation routine is a great help in avoiding the buildup of lactic acid, which is responsible for the formation of trigger points especially after heavy exercising. This routine is intended to assist the lymphatic circulation (chapter 2) and speed up recovery time. For this purpose we will mostly use lots of effleurages, gentle wringings and large thumb or finger kneadings, depending on the area on which you are working.

The recuperation routine is usually applied after exercise. Hydrotherapy (chapter 5) is very useful in this routine, as swollen nodes are very sore to the touch. If an inflammation is present, use cold hydrotherapy to relieve the irritation. Otherwise, if there is no sign of inflammation, use the vascular flush or heat to relieve congestion and assist with circulation of the lymph fluid.

Lymph channels run everywhere in the body but are mostly located along the spine and the deep arteries. Lymph nodes (glands that act as filters to clean bacteria and unwanted particles) are found along the lymph channels. Lymph nodes also are found in patches at the junction of the limbs and the trunk on the inside of the legs.

The recuperation routine should be performed very gently because you are dealing with irritated tissues due to inflamed nerve endings, in response to high levels of lactic acid. Use mostly effleurage moves done lightly with 2 or 3 pounds pressure over the tender areas, and 5 to 7 pounds on thicker muscle groups. When no strong inflammation is present, you can use light vibrations over specific lymph-node areas to effectively decongest and stimulate circulation. Gentle thumb, finger or palmar kneadings can be used to stir up the circulation in thick muscle areas.

Use a light 3 to 5 pounds pressure around the leg joints with small, light, circular effleurages. In a recuperation routine,

drain the lymphatic fluid in the direction of the heart from swollen and inflamed nodes before bringing more fluid to them. Use cold hydrotherapy to soothe nerve endings and cool off the inflammation. If you have to deal with patches of enlarged lymph nodes, apply the swelling technique routine (chapter 8) to decongest them. Start at the periphery of the nodes, using light circular effleurages and drain the nodes from the center toward the outside.

RECUPERATION MASSAGE ROUTINE OUTLINE

Connect with the dog for a few seconds by talking quietly and apply the short version of the relaxation routine.

1. Begin the recuperation routine at the base of the neck, on the left side of the dog. Use effleurages to drain along the entire spine all the way to the croup. Repeat 2 or 3 times.

2. Position yourself halfway between the forelegs and hind legs of your dog. Drain the thorax area with effleurages from the spine downward along the rib cage. Effleurage the first half of the rib cage toward the inside of the foreleg and the second half of the rib cage toward the inside of the hind leg. Repeat each aspect 2 or 3 times. Repeat this work on the other side of the dog.

3. Work the chest with lots of effleurages and kneadings, draining downward between the inside of the foreleg toward the heart. Use gentle shaking moves on the large

9.31 *Recuperation Massage Routine*

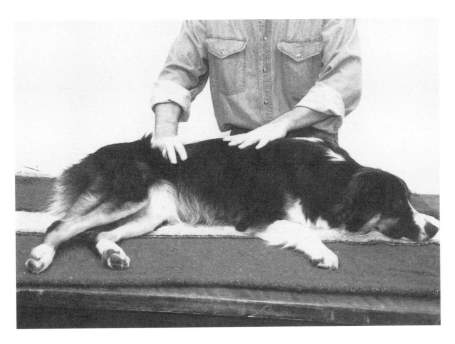

*9.32   **Effleurage of Back:** Recuperation Routine*

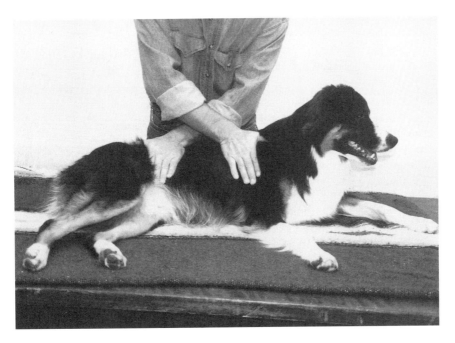

*9.33   **Effleurage of Thorax:** Recuperation Routine*

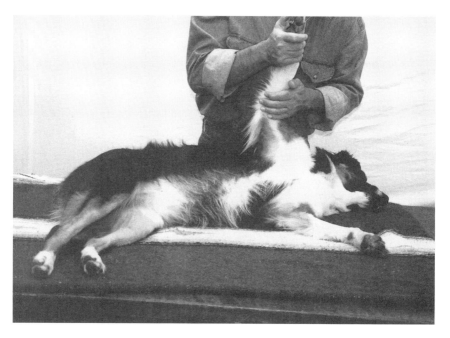

9.34   *Inside Foreleg Effleurage:* *Recuperation Routine*

shoulder muscles. Work the left leg by using effleurages scooping toward the inside leg. Work progressively down the leg draining it upward. Because toxins may be found all the way down to the paw, thoroughly drain the leg up toward the heart. Repeat this work on the right leg.

4. Repeat this procedure on the hind legs. Be gentle when working over the tendons of the lower legs. When working at the back of the dog, move the tail to the side in order to reach the upper attachments of the hamstring muscle groups. Scoop your effleurage movements toward the inside of the leg. If the patches of lymph nodes appear swollen and inflamed in this location, first apply a cold towel to soothe the nerve endings and follow with a gentle swelling technique (chapter 8).

5. Proceed with effleurages over the dog's back, scooping downward onto the chest. Massage all the way to the neck.

6. Spend some extra time draining the base of the skull and the top of the neck behind the poll thoroughly; use gentle muscle squeezings interspersed with effleurages. These moves will help drain the lymph nodes located in the upper neck.

7. Move to the head and drain the area under the jaw along the throat latch and the trachea back toward the neck. To finish this routine and soothe the dog, use a lot of light strokings over the entire body from neck to tail and down the legs.

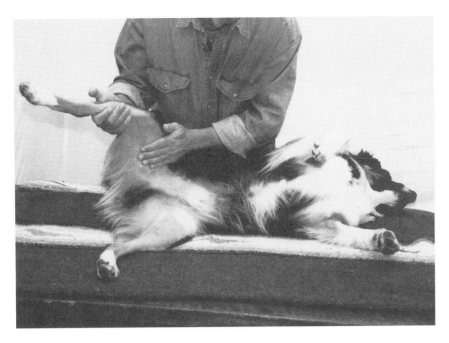

9.35   Inside Hind Leg Effleurage: *Recuperation Routine*

9.36   Neck Effleurage: *Recuperation Routine*

Remember that a dog showing stiffness and some lymphatic inflammation will be fairly sensitive. The sensory nerve endings are tender and will respond quickly to pressure. Be gentle when you start this routine. Constantly check the feedback signs from the dog as you proceed. Pay close attention to what your fingers tell you (see chapter 6 for more on the 4 T's). Your starting pressure should be 1 or 2 pounds. Gently build to between 3 and 5 pounds if the dog appears comfortable. Wrap up by gently stroking the whole body. The recuperation routine should last 15 to 20 minutes.

THE WARM-UP MASSAGE ROUTINE

This routine is designed to stimulate blood circulation in a short period of time to perk up the dog before exercising. The massage will bring more blood, oxygen and nutrients to the muscle fibers. The routine is not a replacement for warm-up exercises, but it is a valuable start nonetheless.

For this routine, use mostly stimulating movements such as shakings, wringings and tapotements interspersed with plenty of effleurages. Perform the routine briskly—but not to the point of irritating the dog—with movements performed at a rhythm of 2 or 3 strokes per second. Your pressure should vary from 5 to 7 pounds in the beginning and up to 10 and 15 pounds when going over large muscle groups. Start gently, and progressively increase the rhythm and pressure of your moves. Remember, the intent is to stir the

blood circulation and perk up the dog, not to spend time performing deep massage on specific muscles.

WARM-UP MASSAGE ROUTINE OUTLINE

Connect with the dog for a few seconds by talking quietly and gently massaging the poll and the upper neck with light muscle squeezings.

1. Begin on the left side of the neck with light shakings and use a gentle rhythm of 1 stroke per second, slowly increasing the pace to 2 or 3 strokes per second. Then switch to wringings, covering the whole neck all the way down to the left shoulder and upper leg. Thoroughly cover all muscles and intersperse with effleurages every 20 to 30 seconds as well as when moving from one body part to another.

2. Thoroughly massage the upper leg both on the inside and outside. Use shakings, wringings, picking-ups and large kneadings interspersed with effleurages. Drain toward the heart, starting from the upper leg and working down with every move. Once at the bottom of the leg, drain the entire leg with 2 long effleurage strokes from the fetlock to the shoulder. Keep your pressure moderate (8 to 12 pounds) and your rhythm swift.

3. Next, massage the chest thoroughly with shakings, muscle squeezings and kneadings, draining the area with effleurages every 20 or 30 seconds.

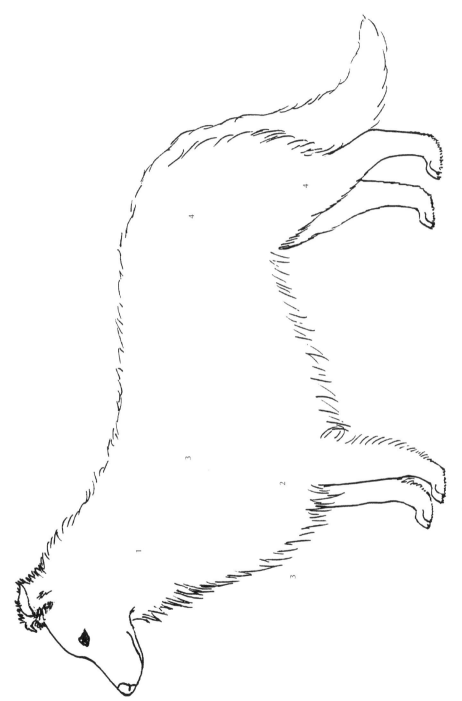

9.37 *Warm-up Massage Routine*

9.38   Fine Shaking Lower Neck: *Warm-up Routine*

9.39   Upper Foreleg Shaking: *Warm-up Routine*

9.40   Chest Shaking: *Warm-up Routine*

9.41   Thorax Shaking: *Warm-up Routine*

Go back over the shoulder with some effleurages or strokings, working your way to the withers. From there, apply wringings across the entire back 2 or 3 times, interspersed with effleurages. Proceed with some tapotements, starting with clappings and then hackings, followed by effleurages. Using shakings, work the entire back and rib cage. Drain toward the heart with effleurages every 20 seconds as you progress. Watch for the feedback signs from the dog. You should slow down the pace as you reach the groin area, because it is a very sensitive area and dogs are naturally very protective of it.

4. Next, go over the large muscle group of the hindquarters and down to the stifle and hock, using shakings, wringings, large palmar kneadings, compressions, all interspersed with effleurages every 20 or 30 seconds. Work the hind leg in the same way as the foreleg. Start from the top, draining it upward as you work your way to the lower aspect of the limb.

Repeat the entire routine on the right side. When you have completed this, apply a gentle wringing over the back and croup followed by effleurages. The routine should last 10 to 15 minutes. Longer sessions of the warm up routine would irritate the dog. Indeed, the size of the dog is an important factor to consider: the more to massage, the longer the routine. Immediately before the exercise, apply the shaking move over the entire legs and the

9.42   Hind Leg Shaking: Warm-up Routine

9.43 Cooldown Massage Routine

large muscles of the shoulder and hindquarters. This will deliver an extra last minute touch to perk up your dog.

COOLDOWN MASSAGE ROUTINE

The purpose of the cooldown routine is to loosen the muscles and generate good blood circulation immediately after exercising so as to prevent stiffening and loss of flexibility. This routine should be applied as soon as the walking cooldown period is finished. In application, the cooldown routine is very close to the warm-up routine, but here the emphasis is on drainage and the relaxation of the muscle groups by using lighter pressure and slower rhythm.

COOLDOWN MASSAGE ROUTINE OUTLINE

1. Start with generous wringings up and down the entire back, 3 to 5 times, interspersed with generous effleurages (15 to 20). Follow with kneadings on the back muscles to relax the tendon attachments along the bones of the spine.

2. Apply larger shakings with some light hackings over the whole rib cage to clear any lactic acid from the deep muscle layers. Follow with effleurages draining toward the heart.

3. Move on to work the hindquarter with wringings, compressions and kneadings, all interspersed with effleurages.

9.44   *Wringing Over Back:* *Cooldown Routine*

9.45 Wringing Over Hindquarter: *Cooldown Routine*

9.46 Effleurage Hind Legs: *Cooldown Routine*

9.47   *Effleurage Forelegs:* *Cooldown Routine*

9.48   *Effleurage of Neck:* *Cooldown Routine*

4. Work the hind legs with large kneadings and effleurages, beginning at the upper aspect of the leg, above the stifle, effleuraging upward. Use 15 to 20 small effleurages until you reach the bottom of the leg, then from the paw, effleurage all the way up the whole leg. Repeat 3 or 4 times to cover all aspects of the leg (inside, outside, front and back). Work both legs.

5. Using several effleurages or strokings, move back to the withers and apply thorough kneadings over the muscle attachments to relax them. Drain the withers thoroughly with effleurages.

6. Move on to work the shoulders and forelegs with wringings, kneadings and pick-ups (on the leg below the elbow), all interspersed with effleurages every 20 or 30 seconds. Drain the forelegs in the same manner as you drained the hind legs. When finished with the legs, use light compressions, kneadings and effleurages to work the chest muscles.

7. Finish this area with thorough wringings up and down the entire neck, followed by large kneadings and muscle squeezings over the crest of the neck. Follow with lots of effleurages.

The overall time of this routine should be less than 20 minutes. It is a good idea to follow the routine with stretching exercises (chapter 4) to help clear and reset the muscles after the workout and cool down routine. If during your work you detect stress or trigger points or other abnormalities, use the appropriate techniques (chapter 8) to remedy the situation. See chapter 10 for the trouble spot routine, which is a nice complement to a maintenance massage routine, especially if your dog exercises regularly.

With practice you will become familiar with each routine and will discover what works best for your dog. You will even be able to create your own variations. Be innovative and try different approaches. When in doubt about the effect of a specific routine, check with your canine massage therapist.

10

To improve the quality of your work you need to know the most common stress sites found in the dog. In this chapter, the following four important body regions will be discussed:

- ❖ head and neck
- ❖ shoulders and forelegs
- ❖ back and rib cage
- ❖ hindquarters

The location of each stress area will be specified, as well as the movements they affect, their signs and symptoms.

Stress sites are those areas where several muscle groups attach. During intense muscular activity, these areas will show tension of varying degrees, ranging from a mild tightness to chronic contracture and eventual spasm.

Many dogs experience reduced muscle action as a result of tight muscles. Because the entire muscle structure of the dog works simultaneously, you will most likely find more than one stress area. In the case

of a recovery from injury, in addition to the actual pain of the injury, you will find compensatory muscle tension in the other limbs and the back and neck.

A thorough knowledge of these stress areas will give you a better appreciation of your dog's fitness and where to apply your massage. The appropriate massage will directly affect your dog's physical performance, allowing for better muscular contraction with more power, a greater flexibility and increased overall coordination.

1. HEAD AND NECK

The head and neck play an important role in the dog's movements. Good flexibility in the neck is vital to performance. A dog uses his head and neck constantly to balance the rest of his body. This is obvious during running—the downward swing of the head will help lift the rear legs off the ground as the dog moves forward. The head and neck are also very active when the dog plays, for example, when catching a stick, a Frisbee or a ball.

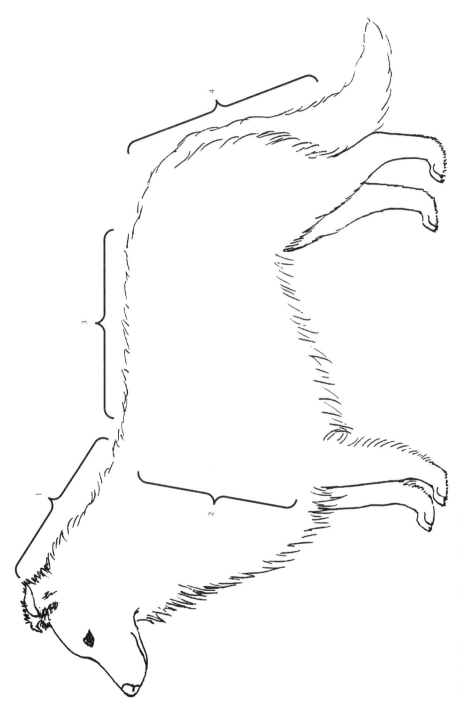

10.1 *Common Stress Sites Chart*

Most neck tension will be found in the extensor muscles (the occipitalis, splenius, rhomboid and trapezius muscles), which are at the back of the head (the poll) and also in front of the withers. When there is tension present in these muscles, the dog may show discomfort by stretching his head downward. When these muscles are tight, the dog may resist downward motion as well as movement to either side.

Upon palpation, you will feel both muscle attachments at the base of the skull and in front of the withers feeling very tense and almost rigid. Sometimes, as a result of the discomfort felt by the dog, compensatory tension will build up in the flexor muscles of the neck (the brachiocephalicus, mastoid and sternohyoidei muscles). Tension in these muscles will be felt along the entire flexor muscles and in front of the shoulder point. The dog will try to stretch his neck by moving his head in the opposite direction of the tension, up and to one side.

Some activities that could cause stress in the neck and head area are guard dog training, obedience, pulling a harness/ cart/sled, agility dog training (obstacles), tracking, guide work for the visually impaired, Frisbee and flyball competition.

2. Shoulders and Forelegs

A strong flexible shoulder and foreleg is essential for proper athletic performance. Good muscle power at the shoulder joint will ensure a high level of performance. This is well demonstrated during jumping

as the dog uses his shoulder and stretches his leg up in front of his body during the jumping.

You may find tension in the latissimus dorsi and triceps muscles and eventually in the biceps brachii. Depending on the intensity of the workout, some tension can be found in the serratus (cervicis and thoracis) muscles that move the scapula back and forth, the supraspinatus and infraspinatus muscles of the scapula, as well as the rhomboids, deltoid and posterior trapezius muscles. The flexor and extensor muscle of the lower leg often show some muscle tension.

When tension is present in these shoulder muscles, the dog loses the flexibility in his shoulder movement resulting in reduced motion, coordination and power. This will also trigger compensation tension to develop in the hindquarters. The shoulder and foreleg muscles might feel tight all along their course with most of their tension at the origin tendon. If that tension develops mostly on one side, the dog will be restricted and show a shorter stride on that side.

Some activities that could cause stress on the shoulder and foreleg are guard dog training, racing, hunting, herding, pulling a harness/cart/sled, tracking, flyball competition, agility competition and guiding the visually impaired.

3. Back and Rib Cage

The vertebral column and the rib cage are made up of bones, ligaments and muscles. The role of the vertebral column is to protect the spinal cord and to provide a solid anchor for strong muscle groups. The role of the rib cage is to protect vital organs, specifically the lungs and heart.

The muscles of the back are the spinalis dorsi, longissimus dorsi, iliocostalis and serratus posterior muscles (both the anterior and posterior part); they contribute to the extension of the back. The external and internal oblique, the rectus abdominus and the intercostal muscles not only stabilize the rib cage and abdomen area during movement but also strongly contribute to the flexion of the back.

When these muscles are tight, the dog will show soreness to a touch on the back and less coordinated power during motion. The dog will eventually show restriction in lateral bending of the opposite side. You might find tension in the forward attachment behind the withers and the backward attachment over the hip area of both the longissimus dorsi and the iliocostalis muscles. Occasionally, a compensatory tension will develop in the intercostal muscles of the rib cage. When there is lots of jumping involved, the abdominal muscles will also show tension by the hip and rib attachments.

Some activities that could cause stress on the back and rib cage are racing, flyball, herding, guard dog training, agility, hunting, pulling a harness/cart/sled and tracking.

4. HINDQUARTERS

The hindquarters are a very important part of the dog's anatomy as they are considered the engine of the dog. The landmarks of the hindquarters that can be palpated are point of croup (ilium), point of buttock (ischium), point of the hip (femur) and stifle joint (femur, tibia and patella).

The bulky muscles of the hindquarters anchor strongly to the lumbar spine and the pelvis. They run downward and attach to the femur and tibia of the hind leg. The muscles that move the femur are the iliacus, the gluteus medius and maximus, the sartorius, the quadriceps femoris and the tensor fascia latae. When these muscles develop tension, the dog shows discomfort in his back with restricted hip motion and shortened leg protraction and retraction.

The muscles that move the tibia are the gastrocnemius, the biceps femoris, the semitendinosus and the semimembranosus. When these muscles show tension, the dog may show lameness, restricted protraction, a loss of power during retraction and eventually a sore back. When the gastrocnemius gets tight, the dog will show discomfort in standing on that leg. You may also find tension along the lumbar and the sacrum sections of the spine where most of the muscle groups attach.

Some activities that could cause stress on the hindquarters and hind legs are agility competition, pulling a harness/cart/sled, hunting, tracking, guard dog training, herding, racing, Frisbee and flyball competition.

GAIT ASSESSMENT

You can train yourself to detect muscular problems by closely watching the actions of your dog when he walks, trots or runs. Assess the length of the strides, the smoothness of execution and the soundness of each step. If your dog is lame in the front leg, he will raise or bob his head as the lame leg strikes the ground. If lame in the hind leg, your dog will drop his head as the lame leg strikes the ground. Any lameness during the walk shows a possible problem in the muscular structure. Generally, lameness during the trot indicates a structural problem (check with your veterinarian).

THE TROUBLE SPOTS ROUTINE

The trouble spots routine is designed to deal with the most commonly occurring trouble spots of the dog, prevent their corresponding stress points from developing and the eventual formation of trigger points. This routine is a nice complement to a maintenance routine especially if your animal exercises regularly. Keep in mind that the following locations are common but not absolute. Always be aware of other potential stress areas which may develop in response to particular training and exercises, or trauma.

If a strong level of inflammation is detected in these areas, first apply the ice cup massage technique (see chapter 5) for a few minutes to decrease the sensitivity of the nerve endings and reduce the inflammation. Then begin your work with the short version of the relaxation routine to calm and prepare the dog. Follow with the trouble spot routine, starting at the neck with the first trouble spot.

1. Work the entire upper neck area where the splenius capitis and the upper rhomboid muscles attach, as well as the ligamentum nuchae attachment at the occiput between the ears and behind the skull. This is an area of constant stress for a dog who engages in strenuous activities. Use the SEW approach from chapter 8 to warm up the whole upper neck. Take the time to relax the muscles fibers in that area with lots of thumb kneadings and gentle finger frictions; this work will prevent the formation of stress points. Then apply some muscle squeezings all along the crest of the neck starting with a 5-pound pressure and progressing to 10 pounds depending on the degree of tension you find; use your judgment. If the area is tender, the dog will react by moving away from the pressure or by arching the neck against your pressure. If you move too quickly into heavier pressure, you may make the existing tension worse. Use the WES approach to drain the neck and flow to the next trouble spot.

2. In the lower aspect of the neck, the next trouble spot is found in the brachiocephalicus muscle. This muscle is involved in the protraction of the foreleg, the head carriage and side movements of the neck and head. If the brachiocephalicus muscle becomes tight, the dog will not be able to carry its head correctly and it will be uncomfortable when circling. Severe tightening of this muscle

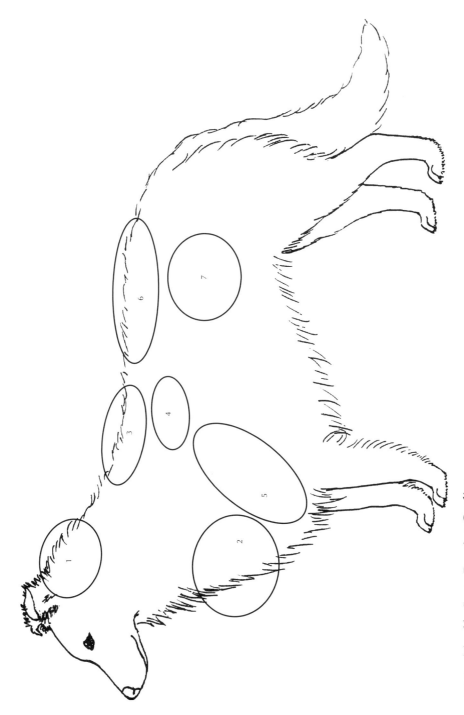

10.2 *Trouble Spots Routine Outline*

results in the dog being off on most of its movements.

When the muscle is tender, the animal will react to light pressure by flinching and pulling away. As you work this area, the dog will most likely relax into the treatment and drop his neck and shoulder on the same side you are treating.

To massage this area, start with the SEW approach over the neck from top to bottom. Then apply kneadings to loosen the muscle fibers and prevent the formation of stress points. Follow with some gentle cross-fiber frictions over the whole length of the muscle. Intersperse with thorough effleurages to drain the area. Then apply gentle compressions to the entire length of the muscle. Follow with the WES approach to drain the neck thoroughly and finish with some light strokings to flow to the next trouble spot.

3. The withers area is the skeletal attachment site for the rhomboid and the trapezius muscles, which are directly involved in the movement of the scapula. The repetitive movement of any gait and the stress of a potentially difficult maneuver (for example, the impact of landing after a jump) in combination with poor footing can cause irritation of the muscle attachment onto the withers.

As you reach this area with strokings, move on to warm up the muscles with the SEW approach.

Then use gentle muscle squeezings (5 to 10 pounds of pressure) to assess the degree of inflammation or irritation. Thoroughly drain the area with lots of effleurages, use kneadings to loosen the muscle fibers, then drain with effleurages again. Apply gentle friction across the length of the fibers starting gently with moderate pressure and rhythm, working progressively deeper for a period of 2 minutes. This will prevent the formation of stress points. Intersperse with effleurages every 20 seconds to drain the area as you work. Keep track of time to avoid overworking the fibers. Follow with the WES approach to ensure a generous drainage. Finish with light strokings and move over to check the fourth trouble spot.

4. The forward attachment of the longissimus dorsi is located behind the withers a few inches down from the top of the withers. Irritation and inflammation of this area can result from an extensive workout. When this area is irritated, tension can be felt in one or both sides of this muscle and will eventually lead to the formation of stress points. Take time to warm up the area with the SEW approach over the whole muscle. Then use kneadings to relax the muscle fibers and follow with some gentle finger frictions to prevent the formation of stress points. If sore, the dog will probably flinch, arch his back or move away from your pressure—the degree of reaction is

indicative of the amount of inflammation present. If you detect a strong level of inflammation, apply the ice cup massage technique described in chapter 5 for a few minutes to decrease the sensitivity of the nerve endings while reducing the inflammation. Follow with light finger frictions along the entire muscle to loosen its fibers and intersperse with effleurages every 20 seconds. When finished, use the WES approach to thoroughly drain the whole muscle and then use light strokings to move to the next trouble spot.

5. The supraspinatus muscle is one of the most important muscles of the shoulder; it works in conjunction with the infraspinatus, the deltoid and the teres major. These muscles serve to prevent lateral dislocation of the shoulder. The supraspinatus is directly involved in lateral movements such as abduction (as the agonist muscle) and adduction (as the antagonist muscle) of the foreleg. Abrupt changes of direction to the sides (such as in herding, agility competition and flyball games) renders the infraspinatus very susceptible to strain. When the muscle is soar, the dog will exhibit signs of lameness and restricted movement in the foreleg on the same side.

Start massaging this area with the SEW approach. The dog may flinch or, if feeling very tender, will move away from your pressure. So start working lightly with lots of

effleurages and wringings to warm up the area. Then apply light kneadings to relax the muscle fibers and follow with effleurages. Friction the entire muscle, back and forth for 2 minutes to loosen its fibers; this will prevent the formation of stress points. Intersperse with effleurages every 20 seconds. Follow with gentle compressions to the entire length of the muscle and finish with the WES approach to thoroughly drain the entire muscle. Use strokings to move to the next trouble spot.

6. The longissimus dorsi (back attachment) and the gluteus maximus muscle join in this area, which is most often found to be a very sensitive or even tender area. Start massaging the area delicately with the SEW approach. When the area is inflamed or knotted, the dog will sink or sag in response to your pressure. Apply the ice massage technique first to numb the nerve endings of the area you are treating. Then stimulate the circulation thoroughly with wringings and gentle compressions. Intersperse with effleurages every 20 seconds. Use kneadings to relax the muscles fibers. Follow with light frictions along the entire muscles to prevent the formation of stress points. Thoroughly drain the area with effleurages. Apply palmar compressions along the length of the whole muscles to complete the treatment. Finish with the WES approach to thoroughly drain the area. Use

light strokings to move to the next trouble spot.

7. The hip attachment of the tensor fascia latae (TFL) area just below the point of the hip is a critical spot. This is where both the TFL muscle and the iliacus muscle attach. These two muscles are strong hip flexors. Furthermore the TFL muscle plays a role in extending the stifle during retraction of the hind leg.

When this trouble spot is stressed, the dog will show discomfort on the same side when turning and will tend to throw his leg outward during protraction. Be careful and very gentle when starting to work this area. If the area appears very tender at first touch, use the ice massage technique prior to the treatment to numb the nerve endings. Stir up the circulation in the area with the SEW approach.

Apply compressions with a moderate to heavy pressure (5 to 12 pounds) along the TFL muscle. Then use kneadings to relax the muscle fibers of this muscle and intersperse with effleurages. Apply cross-fiber frictions over the entire muscle to prevent the formation of stress points. Alternate with effleurages every 20 seconds. After the massage, apply cold to ease the nerve endings and flush the blood circulation in that area. Finish with the WES approach to thoroughly drain the area.

A general stretching of the dog (see chapter 4) is particularly good to complete this routine. After the massage, active exercise for the dog is a good follow-up, but keep any lateral work (circles) to a minimum at first, especially if the shoulder and TFL muscles were tight. To finish the routine, apply lots of light strokings over the entire dog's body to give it a sense of relaxation.

11

Massage can assist your dog during recovery from various injuries or common problems. Always consult your veterinarian for proper diagnosis in any situation and be sure to check the list of contraindications listed in chapter 1 before applying massage.

Allergies   A relaxation routine will ease your dog during allergic reactions. Massaging the outside of the elbow (where the biceps joins the forearm) is recommended in Chinese massage.

Arthritis and rheumatism   Common in geriatric dogs, arthritis and rheumatism mostly affect the hips, lower spine, hock and knees, and to a lesser degree the shoulder and elbow. Massage won't cure arthritis or rheumatism, but it will relieve the pain and muscle tension caused by such conditions. Massage will break the "pain-tension-more pain" cycle in the affected limb as well as the opposing limbs that bear the weight of compensation. Massage contributes to slowing down the degenerative process caused by such a condition. Try to massage early in the morning to loosen the structure involved

as well as in the evening to relieve the tension buildup and the soreness. Chinese massage suggests kneading the outside of the elbow and just above and in front of the heel on the hind leg to promote good general metabolism and fight off arthritis and rheumatism.

Asthma   A relaxation routine will ease your dog during an asthmatic episode, but a full body maintenance massage is contraindicated at this time. Chinese massage suggests rubbing (kneading) the front paws just above the wrist.

Back problems   Occurring in any breed, back problems such as slipped disk, sponylosis, muscle pain and spasm are seen mostly in the long-backed dogs like Dachshunds, Beagles, Basset Hounds, Poodles, and others. The symptoms are a sudden onset of soreness or pain ranging from reluctance to get up and walk to full-blown hind leg paralysis. You should first see your veterinarian to rule out nerve involvement, fractures, a prolapsed disk, or other problems. Massage will help relieve some of the pain and muscle tension resulting from this condition on the hind legs, the forelegs, the back and neck. Focus your massage on the back region, especially the thoracolumbar (TL) junction area and the lumbosacral (LS) junction, as well as the rest of the hind legs.

Chinese massage   Chinese massage, also known as acupressure, is a particular form of massage, close to what is presented in this book, except that it differs in its application. Chinese massage emphasizes the application of small pressures on specific areas or point locations that are part of a network of so called "meridians," which are believed to carry "vital" energy to specific areas and organs of the body.

Collapsing trachea   Most common in small and toy breeds where the cartilaginous rings of the trachea are abnormally weak or improperly formed. When the dog starts to breathe quickly due to exertion or excitement, the vacuum created causes the trachea to collapse resulting in coughing, stertorous breathing, neck extension and anxiety. Massaging the ventral (underneath) aspect of the neck will be beneficial in relieving this problem promptly.

Digestive problems   Do not apply a full body massage while the dog is sick— a light relaxation routine will soothe your dog later. You may consider, however, a gentle kneading of the area just below the knee on the outside of the shinbone as in Chinese massage to soothe this condition.

Fractures   Due to the immobilization of the limb while in the cast, there will be muscle atrophy (wasting). Massage after the cast is removed will promote muscle recovery. Massage of the other limbs and the rest of the body both before and after removal of the cast will lessen compensation tension, increase circulation, stimulate pain-releasing endorphins and ease the dog's overall discomfort.

Hip dysplasia   This malformation of the hip joint is a fairly common problem in all breeds, but especially in large fast-growing breeds of dogs. This condition is due to a poor coxofemoral joint conformation. Drugs and surgery for hip replacement are the only alternatives for this type of problem. Massage will assist in relieving pain and muscle tension in the affected side, as well as in other areas of the body due to compensation. Focus your massage on the lower back and gluts, as well as the quadriceps and hamstring group of muscles. Try to massage early in the morning to loosen the structure involved, as well as in the evening to relieve the tension buildup and the soreness.

Luxating patella   This condition can occur in any dog, but is most commonly seen in toy breeds (Poodle, Bichon Frise, Lhasa Apso, and others). In small breeds, the patella normally luxates medially (inside). If the dog is active, the knee can lock and the quadriceps muscle group can go into contracture and possibly spasm. Massage will help relieve some of the pain and muscle tension resulting from this condition. Focus your massage on the affected leg, as well as the back region due to the compensation.

Osteochondrosis Dissecans (OCD) This condition is common in young, fast-growing, large-breed dogs and is an effect of the articular cartilage, mostly seen in the shoulder, hock, stifle and elbow. The dog will show moderate pain and lameness in the affected leg. The pain may be mild but tends to be continuous. Massage will ease the tension and pain throughout the body including both the affected and opposite (compensating) limbs.

Panosteitis   Also known as growing pains, this condition is seen mostly in young, fast-growing, large-breed dogs. The condition involves the inflammation of the long bones (humerus, radius, femur and tibia) and mostly occurs between the ages of six and 18 months. It shows up as a shifting lameness that affects one or more legs for a variable duration (a few days or weeks). The dog needs lots of rest and perhaps anti-inflammatory medication prescribed by your veterinarian. Massage cannot help this condition directly, but indirectly it can soothe compensation muscle tension and relieve the dog of his soreness. Be cautious when working on the affected limb because any pressure at all on the affected bone is very painful. The rest of the body can be massaged normally.

Post surgery   Light massage will assist and promote muscle recovery as well as relax and comfort your dog. Do not work on the injury site until it is well into the chronic stage; check with your veterinarian. During convalescence, regular massage will prevent compensatory tension from developing in other muscles of the body.

Ununited anconeal (elbow) process and fragmented coronoid (jaw) process   Both conditions, uncommon problems in young dogs, are more often seen in German Shepherds and require surgical correction. Massage can help during convalescence after surgery.

12

BREED-SPECIFIC STRESS SITES

In this chapter we list the most common breeds of dog in North America and the parts of their bodies to emphasize during a massage. If your dog is a mixed-breed, go through the list and choose the breed(s) that best matches your dog's body type. For example, for a short-legged hound with a long back, refer to the Basset Hound listing.

Before you begin massaging your dog, be sure no contraindications exist (see chapter 1). If in doubt, consult your veterinarian.

Always start your massage with a relaxation massage routine (see chapter 9). Continue with a maintenance massage routine and emphasize the areas listed for your dog's breed.

Breed	Weight in lbs. (approx.)	Areas to Emphasize with Massage
Afghan Hound	50–60	neck, shoulders, back
Airedale	45–50	hindquarters, hip area
Akita	75–85	back, hindquarters
Alaskan Malamute	75–85	hindquarters, hip area
American Bulldog	60–120	shoulders, chest, hindquarters
Australian Cattle Dog	30–50	neck, chest, hindquarters
Australian Shepherd	40–50	lower back, hip area
Basenji	20–23	hips, flanks
Basset Hound	40–55	neck, entire back, limbs
Beagle	20–35	neck, shoulders, back
Bearded Collie	40–60	neck, back

BREED	WEIGHT IN LBS. (APPROX.)	AREAS TO EMPHASIZE WITH MASSAGE
Bedlington Terrier	25–40	neck, back, abdomen
Belgian Sheepdog	40–55	neck, back, hindquarters, hips
Bernese Mountain Dog	60–80	back, hip area
Bichon Frise	12–20	neck, back
Bloodhound	60–80	neck, back
Border Collie	40–50	neck, shoulders, lower back
Border Terrier	12–14	hips, hindquarters, stifles
Borzoi	75–105	neck, back, hip area
Boston Terrier	15–25	shoulders, chest, back
Bouvier des Flandres	80–110	shoulders, neck, hindquarters
Boxer	50–70	neck, back, hindquarters
Brittany	25–40	back
Bull Terrier	40–60	neck, lower back, hips
Cairn Terrier	20–30	jaw, neck, back, hips, flanks
Cavalier King Charles Spaniel	10–20	back, hips
Chesapeake Bay Retriever	55–75	back, hindquarters
Chihuahua	2–6	neck, shoulders, hindquarters, stifles
Chow Chow	50–60	back, hindquarters, stifles
Cocker Spaniel	20–30	neck, back, hip area
Collie	40–65	back, hips, flanks, abdomen
Dachshund	10–25	neck, back, hips, hindquarters
Dalmatian	40–45	back, hindquarters
Doberman Pinscher	50–70	back, foreleg, shoulders, hindquarters
English Bulldog	40–50	neck, chest, back
English Setter	50–70	shoulders, back, hindquarters
English Springer Spaniel	25–50	back, hindquarters
English Toy Spaniel	9–12	back, hindquarters
Finnish Spitz	50–80	neck, chest, back
Flat-Coated Retriever	60–70	back, hindquarters
Foxhound	30–50	neck, back

Breed	Weight in lbs. (approx.)	Areas to Emphasize with Massage
Fox Terrier	17–20	neck, shoulders, lower back
French Bulldog	22–28	back, chest, hips
German Shepherd Dog	60–85	back, hip area
German Shorthaired Pointer	45–70	back, hindquarters
Golden Retriever	55–75	neck, back, hip area
Gordon Setter	60–80	shoulders, back, hindquarters
Great Dane	100–150	back, hip area, hindquarters
Great Pyrenees	80–110	back, hindquarters
Greyhound	60–70	neck, withers, back, hip area
Griffon	15–35	neck, shoulders, back
Hovawart	66–88	back, hindquarters
Irish Setter	45–70	forelegs, shoulders, back
Irish Wolfhound	80–110	back, hip area, hindquarters
Jack Russell Terrier	10–20	back, hindquarters
Keeshond	30–40	back, hindquarters
Kerry Blue Terrier	30–40	back, hindquarters
Labrador Retriever	55–75	forelegs, back, hip area
Lakeland Terrier	15–20	chest, back, hindquarters
Leonberger	90–120	back, hindquarters
Lhasa Apso	10–15	back, abdomen
Maltese	5–7	back
Mastiff	90–150	neck, back, hindquarters
Miniature Pinscher	6–10	shoulders, chest, back
Newfoundland	120–150	back, hip area, hindquarters
Norwegian Elkhound	40–60	neck, back, hindquarters
Nova Scotia Duck Tolling Retriever	35–50	back, hindquarters
Old English Sheepdog	80–100	neck, back, hindquarters
Papillon	8–15	back
Pekingese	10–14	neck, back
Pomeranian	5	neck, shoulders, hind legs

BREED	WEIGHT IN LBS. (APPROX.)	AREAS TO EMPHASIZE WITH MASSAGE
Poodle (miniature)	12–25	neck, shoulders, back, hind legs
Poodle (standard)	35–50	foreleg, back, hip area
Poodle (toy)	12–15	neck, back, hindquarters
Portuguese Water Dog	35–60	forelegs, back, hindquarters
Pug	14–18	neck, back, hind legs
Rhodesian Ridgeback	55–65	back, hindquarters
Rottweiler	110	back, hip area
Saint Bernard	100–200	lower back, hips, hind legs
Saluki	45–60	hip area, hindquarters
Samoyed	35–60	back, hindquarters
Schnauzer (giant)	70–90	shoulders, back, hindquarters
Schnauzer (miniature)	12–15	neck, flank, hindquarters
Schnauzer (standard)	35–55	back, hindquarters
Scottish Terrier	20	neck, back, hindquarters
Shetland Sheepdog	20–35	back, hindquarters
Shih Tzu	12–20	neck, back, hindquarters
Siberian Husky	35–60	neck, back, hindquarters
Vizsla	50–65	neck, back, hindquarters
Weimaraner	60–80	back, flanks, hindquarters
Welsh Corgi	15–25	neck, shoulders, back, hindquarters
Welsh Terrier	15–25	neck, hindquarters
West Highland White Terrier	12–20	neck, jaw, back, flanks, hindquarters
Wheaten Terrier	30–40	back, hindquarters
Whippet	15–25	shoulder, back, hindquarters
Yorkshire Terrier	4–15	back, hindquarters

ACTIVITIES

Like the human athlete, an active dog will develop extra muscular tension as a result of increased activity or participation in sports. The following chart lists the most popular activities and the corresponding areas of tension that result from those activities. Those areas should be emphasized during massage.

Remember, all muscle groups work at once, and consequently you will find more than one area of muscular tension. See chapter 10 for the most common stress sites found in active dogs, and a trouble spot massage routine that will help keep muscular stress to a minimum. Regular massage will ensure your dog's fitness and top performance.

ACTIVITIES	AREAS OF MUSCULAR TENSION
Agility	chest, forelegs, back, hindquarters
Earthdog Trials	neck, back, hindquarters
Draft Dog	neck, shoulders, chest, back, hindquarters
Field Trials (Pointers)	neck, shoulders, back
Field Trials (Retrievers)	neck, shoulders, back, limbs
Flyball	neck, back, hindquarters
Frisbee Catching	neck, forelegs, back, hindquarters
Scent Hurdle Dog	neck, back, hindquarters
Schutzhund	neck, shoulders, chest, back, hip area, limbs
Sledding	neck, shoulders, chest, back, limbs
Herding	neck, back, limbs
Tracking	neck, shoulders, chest
Water Rescue	neck, shoulders, chest, limbs

13

RECORD KEEPING

Keeping a record of your massage work and your findings after each massage treatment is as important as keeping records of your dog's visits to the veterinarian.

Your records should contain the following:

❖ History and background information (to the best of your knowledge) on your dog, including, for example, previous ownership, past accidents or injuries, and type of training, if applicable.

❖ Personality traits like playfulness, shyness, hyperactivity, calmness, nastiness when in cage, biting, and so on.

❖ Medication(s), if any.

❖ Type of training the dog is involved in at the present time, plus his tendencies during training, like problems with bending, jumping, picking up, galloping, and so on.

❖ Note the overall condition of your dog at the time of each massage. List any stress points, trigger points, inflammations, swellings and the findings of your 4 T's.

❖ If your dog gets hurt (either in training or at play), record what happened, how and when, as well as the location of the injury on the dog. Also note the treatment given at the time.

❖ When using equipment on your dog (for example, a harness), record when and how the dog responded to the change over the following 7 to 10 days.

This information will help you appreciate how well your dog responds to your massage treatments. By keeping thorough notes, you will be able to track any changes in the symptoms he shows. Also, you will be able to give your veterinarian the kind of clinical information needed to help your dog.

CASE STUDY

Name: _Digger_
Breed: _Australian Shepherd_
Colour: _Black Tri_
Size: _Medium_
Weight: _105 lbs_
Born: _____ Age: _10 yrs_
Markings: _Black, tan with white_
Discipline: _Herding_

Canine Massage Awareness
P.O. Box 39003
RPO Billings Bridge
Ottawa Ontario K1H 1A1
Tel (613)-737-9846
Fax (613)-737-9213
CMA is a division of M.A. Inc.

Owner: _Lynn Alau_
Address: _P.O. Box 60_
North Bay, Ontario
Tel: _(705) 619-2838_
Kennel: _Dream Quest_
Tel: _as above._
Vet: _Dr. D. Corbett_
Tel: _(705) 789-9246_
Date: _Oct 3/97_

Conditioning: ☐ Low ☐ Moderate ☑ High ☐ Overweight ☐ Underweight

Major complaint: What, Where, When, How: _Has become less enthusiastic about working. Has slight limp - not moving freely. Dr. suggested muscle tight in (L) shoulder._

History of present illness: _X-rays report - clear by vet - no other apparent cause for discomfort_

History of past illness(es): _Fell down stairs when playing - June/97_

Examination/palpation: _Tension in Brachiocephalicus (L) - Stress points found (L) Supraspinat and Latissimus Dorsi - close to shoulder. Tension also found in Iliocostalis (L), Stoid (Rt) and Gluteus medius (Rt)_

Treatment: _Relaxation routine, check-up for Stress points, (Maintenance routine before checking for S.P.'s) Emphasized kneading, friction + drainage. O/E techn. (L) Shoulder. Stretched neck + legs._

Maintenance Program: _perform exercises as shown - SEW/OES twice a day for 4 days, then once a day + after every large workout - general stretching._

13.1   Case Study Sample

Knowing your dog well will assist you in determining the best maintenance massage program for him. With the practice of regular massage, you will be aware of signs and symptoms that indicate your dog needs veterinary attention much sooner than you would with the usual practice of grooming. You will never look at or touch your dog the same way again.

I·N·D·E·X